HIGHLY EFFECTIVE HABITS

HIGHLY EFFECTIVE HABITS

140+ TINY LITTLE TRICKSI

Sasha Zeven

ORIGAMI EDITIONS
READING FOR BETTER LIVING

EASY WINS SERIES

Published by Origami Editions

www.origamieditions.com

© Copyright 2025 - All rights reserved.

P-ISBN 978-1-968412-00-5 (Paperback)
P-ISBN 978-1-968412-01-2 (Hardcover)

E-ISBN 978-1-968412-02-9

The best time to plant a tree was 20 years ago.
The second-best time is now.

— *Chinese proverb*

FREE BONUS!

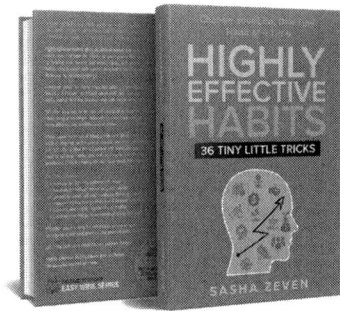

As a valued reader and to thank you for your purchase, we invite you to download a complimentary eBook featuring 36 additional Highly Effective Habits that complement this edition.

Scan the QR code below, subscribe to the **Origami Editions** newsletter, and access your free copy in less than 2 minutes.

You will also occasionally receive curated self-development tools, updates on upcoming releases, exclusive offers, and resources to support your personal and professional growth journey.

Reading for Better Living.

CONTENTS

INTRODUCTION   **17**

TIME   **21**

Morning Routines: Starting the day with clarity and energy   **23**

    Planning: Review Your Planning at Least Twice   23
    Productivity: Find Your Golden Window   24
    Recharging: Indulge in Calming Rituals of Your Choice   25

Prioritization: Focusing on what truly matters   **26**

    Planning: Focus on What Truly Matters   26
    Productivity: Budget Your Time for Projects   27
    Recharging: Treat Your Personal Time as Your Professional Time 28

Evening Wind Down: Creating closure and restful transitions   **29**

    Planning: First Trust What You Want to Achieve   29
    Productivity: Learn How to Take a Step Back and Strategize   30
    Recharging: Automate Your Sunset Rituals   31

Time Blocking: Structuring your day intentionally   **32**

    Planning: Create a "Weekly Flow Map" with Daily Themes   32
    Productivity: Benefit Fully from Your Golden Window   33
    Recharging: Gamify Goals to Achieve Them   34

Delegation & Saying No: Freeing space and mental load   **35**

    Planning: Design Your "Let-Go Board"   35
    Productivity: Tag Incoming Tasks and Duties   36
    Recharging: Delegation Dice   37

Optimization: Doing more with less effort   **38**

    Planning: Organize Your Calendar to Look Like Tetris   38
    Productivity: The Two-Tap System   39
    Recharging: Double Up to Optimize Effects   40

Deep Work: Techniques for focused work   **41**

  Planning: Use Focus Planning Cards   41
  Productivity: Optimize Time-Efficiency with the Pomodoro Technique   42
  Recharging: Reset Your Brain with the Eyes, Air, Away Method   43

Efficiency Tools: Using calendars, task managers, and automation   **44**

  Planning: Use AI to Triage Your To-Do List   44
  Productivity: Automate Recurring Tasks Using Technology   45
  Recharging: Become Emotionally Aware   46

FINANCE   **49**

Budgeting & Tracking: Awareness of inflow and outflow   **51**

  Earning/Spending: Maintain a Personal Profit & Loss Statement   51
  Investing: Match Purchases with a Proportional Investment   52
  Mindset/Impact: Write Your Money Principles   53

Emergency Fund: Security and peace of mind   **54**

  Earning/Spending: Dedicate One Skill to One Bill   54
  Investing: Invest the Round-Ups   55
  Mindset/Impact: Audit Your Personal Liquidity Level   56

Smart Spending: Needs vs wants, conscious consumerism   **57**

  Earning/Spending: Spend Money on What Makes You Truly Happy   57
  Investing: Invest in Expenses Supporting Your Lifestyle   58
  Mindset/Impact: Upgrade Purchases Once to Never Regret   59

Future Success: Simple, long-term investing strategies   **60**

  Earning/Spending: One-Month Business Tester   60
  Investing: Scout for Micro-Investment in New Trends   61
  Mindset/Impact: Compete Around Passive Income with Your Friends   62

Income Diversification: Side hustles, passive income   **63**

  Earning/Spending: Invest in Yourself   63
  Investing: Invest in Royalty Businesses   64
  Mindset/Impact: Use Crowdfunding to Leverage Investment   65

Debt Management: Avoiding and reducing toxic debt   **66**

  Earning/Spending: Use a Side Hustle to Cover Debts   66
  Investing: Invest Saving Accruals in Trends Research   67
  Mindset/Impact: Understand Your Debt Fully   68

Minimalism & Value: Buying for function and joy   **69**

    Earning/Spending: Control the Types of Purchases You Make   69
    Investing: Spend on What Can Earn You Money   70
    Mindset/Impact: Step Back to Control Impulsive Purchases   71

Giving & Generosity: Money as a tool for impact   **72**

    Earning/Spending: Offer What Served You   72
    Investing: Invest in Causes You Trust   73
    Mindset/Impact: Give Without Expecting Anything in Return   74

MENTAL   77

Present-moment: Awareness and mindfulness practices   **79**

    Mindfulness: Be Present in the Moment   79
    Beliefs: Prove Your Self-Limiting Beliefs Wrong   80
    Learning: Break Your Routines   81

Journaling: Reflection and self-discovery   **82**

    Mindfulness: Understand Daily Life Patterns   82
    Beliefs: Be Driven by Who You Want to Become   83
    Learning: Collect Life Lessons and Let Them Shape You   84

Stress Management: Coping mechanisms and calming techniques   **85**

    Mindfulness: Prepare for Stressful Situations   85
    Beliefs: Free Yourself from Self-Bias Systems   86
    Learning: Identify Stress Symptoms and Ease Them   87

Growth Mindset: Embracing change and learning   **88**

    Mindfulness: Apply the 3 Ps   88
    Beliefs: Grow Empowering Beliefs   89
    Learning: Learn From Your Proximity Circle   90

Decluttering the Mind: Reducing noise and negative inputs   **91**

    Mindfulness: Reduce the Pace to Think Clearly   91
    Beliefs: Remove Self-Limiting Beliefs and Transform Yourself   92
    Learning: Keep the Learning Circle Alive   93

Self-Talk & Inner Dialogue: Reframing beliefs   **94**

    Mindfulness: Develop Situational Analytic Skills   94
    Beliefs: Challenge Your Self-Limiting Beliefs   95
    Learning: Acknowledge Challenges to Better Overcome Them   96

Mental Boundaries: Detaching from drama or negativity   **97**

    Mindfulness: Know How to Protect Your Emotions   97
    Beliefs: Build Emotional Boundaries   98
    Learning: Target Your Learnings   99

Curiosity: Feeding the mind with questions and wonder   **100**

    Mindfulness: Handle Conflictual Interaction with Wisdom   100
    Beliefs: Map Out Your Beliefs   101
    Learning: Track Your Curiosity and Feed It   102

PHYSICAL   105

Light Activity: Walking, stretching, daily movement   **107**

    Movement: Avoid Office Syndrome   107
    Nutrition: Drink-Then-Do, Stretch-Then-Snack   108
    Health: Listen to Your Body   109

Physical Routine: Strength, endurance, or flexibility   **110**

    Movement: Repeat Consistently to Beat Intensity   110
    Nutrition: Be Intentional in Choosing What You Eat   111
    Health: Develop Mind Clarity and Memory by Sleeping Well   112

Sleep Hygiene: Deep, restorative sleep   **113**

    Movement: Use Gravity to Exercise Lightly   113
    Nutrition: Prepare Your Mind for a Restful Night   114
    Health: Breathe Properly to Enhance Sleeping   115

Breathing & Posture: Oxygen and alignment   **116**

    Movement: Maintain Healthy Postures   116
    Nutrition: Eat with Your Breathing in Mind   117
    Health: Keep Your Spine Healthy   118

Nature: Recharging through natural elements   **119**

    Movement: Connect With Nature Through Meditation   119
    Nutrition: Connect With Nature as Often as Possible   120
    Health: Meditate to Self-Diagnosis How Your Body Feels   121

Limiting Substances: Alcohol, sugar, stimulants   **122**

    Movement: Combine Consistency and Intensity   122
    Nutrition: Anticipate Your Craving Weaknesses   123
    Health: Practice Abstinence   124

Rest & Recovery: Scheduling downtime   **125**

    Movement: Stretch Your Body Every Day   125
    Nutrition: Maintain an Evening Ritual   126
    Health: Impose Screen Fasting day on Yourself   127

Balance & Coordination: Staying agile and body-aware   **128**

    Movement: Exercise Your Balance   128
    Nutrition: Eat to Strengthen Your Balance   129
    Health: Exercise Movement Coordination   130

SOCIAL   133

Active Listening: Presence in conversations   **135**

    Love: Develop Mutual Emotional Awareness   135
    Family: Encourage and Practice Freedom of Expression   136
    Friendship: Develop Active Listening   137

Kindness Rituals: Small daily acts for others   **138**

    Love: Demonstrate Meaningful, Loving Attention   138
    Family: Think About Others, Not Just Yourself   139
    Friendship: Use Humor to Strengthen Social Connection   140

Quality Time: Prioritizing meaningful relationships   **141**

    Love: Disconnect to Reconnect with Others   141
    Family: Develop the Art of Teaching   142
    Friendship: Strengthen Friendship With 1-on-1 Meetings   143

Networking & Connection: Building bridges, not walls   **144**

    Love: Socialize With Other Couples   144
    Family: Care for Neighborly Relationships   145
    Friendship: Surround Yourself with Growth-Minded People   146

Support Systems: Knowing when and how to lean   **147**

    Love: Exercise Emotional Intelligence   147
    Family: Set Healthy Boundaries   148
    Friendship: Use Your Network to Support Your Life   149

Conflict Management: Emotional maturity   **150**

    Love: Develop a Conflict No-Go List   150
    Family: Develop Emotional Maturity   151
    Friendship: Don't Weight Yourself With Passive Resentments   152

Mentorship & Giving Back: Sharing wisdom — 153

Love: Invest in Growing People Around You — 153
Family: Connect With Other Generations to Keep Learning — 154
Friendship: Use Your Social Circle to Develop Yourself — 155

Community Participation: Being part of something bigger — 156

Love: Give Back Using Your Skills — 156
Family: Cultivate Healthy Values — 157
Friendship: Contribute Meaningfully to Benefit the Local Community — 158

PASSION — 161

Creative Expression: Art, writing, music, or building — 163

Exploration: Remain Curious About New Hobbies — 163
Practice: Commit to Repetitive Free Expression — 164
Development: Develop a Growth Mindset in Creativity — 165

Self-Discovery: Understanding your unique identity and needs — 166

Exploration: Start Small at Low-Stakes — 166
Practice: Collect Inspiring Samples — 167
Development: Stay Close to Who You Are — 168

Playfulness: Doing things for fun and joy — 169

Exploration: Be Curious About Unusual Creative Hobbies — 169
Practice: Develop Self-Confidence Through Performances — 170
Development: Play Board Games to Exercise Your Brain — 171

Vision Crafting: Dreaming big with clarity — 172

Exploration: Run Idea Incubator Sessions — 172
Practice: Model Ideas Before Executing Them — 173
Development: Use Reverse Thinking in Project Planning — 174

Creative Expression: Making space to express yourself freely — 175

Exploration: Nurture Instinctive Creativity — 175
Practice: Use Focus to Create — 176
Development: Model Successful People to Find Your Own Style — 177

Flow Activities: Doing what absorbs you so profoundly that you lose track of time — 178

Exploration: Reconnect With Childhood Passions — 178
Practice: Allow Curiosity to Lead Learning — 179
Development: Trick Your Brain for Creative Efficiency — 180

Passion Sharing: Inspiring others by sharing what excites and energizes you   **181**

    Exploration: Create a Feedback Circle   181
    Practice: Document and Share Your Learning Process   182
    Development: Teach What You Love   183

Passion Rituals: Creating recurring moments that keep your passion alive   **184**

    Exploration: Diversify Your Environment to Create   184
    Practice: Let Earth Inspire Your Expression   185
    Development: Allow Yourself to Reset   186

INTRODUCTION

J ohn Lennon once said,
"Life is what happens to you while you're busy making other plans."

This pithy quote resonated with his fans and haters alike across the world. To those who may have doubted the statement's truth, Lennon's unexpected assassination in 1980 only seemed to drive the point further home.

Fast forward nearly half a century, and this saying holds more truth than ever. People from all over the world will tell you that one of life's defining qualities is capriciousness. Its unpredictability. Its refusal to fall in line with our plans and dreams.

Bracing for impact, is the way you're living now really all you can do?

Or do you have more power than you think?

If you've picked up this book, I'll assume you think that there's more to you. You want to believe you're in control. You want to believe you possess the power to influence events to shape your life the way you want. John Lennon's quote may sound nice over a dinner party with your friends, but it's pretty glum when you think about it. I mean, what's the point of making all those plans and goals if life is going to play its own game in the end anyway? What's the point of working towards a goal? Hell, what's the point of *anything*? Surely, the truth must be different. Surely, there must be a way to turn the tables on life and make it do our bidding.

I have good news for you.

There is a way.

Of course, I'm not selling you a magic potion that will grant you mastery over your destiny or guarantee you achieve your wildest wishes. I'm not giving you a magic lamp with a genie inside it. Such things don't exist; we all know that. What I propose through this book are inspiring ways to reclaim control over your life and see marked improvements in a very short time. What are these ways, you ask?

It is the way of habits.

As per the Oxford Dictionary, a habit is "a settled or regular tendency or practice, especially one that is hard to give up." You may not know it, but your habits define your life. They govern every waking moment of your existence. It is your habits that decide where you'll be five, ten, or even fifteen years from now. Heck, your habits can even influence what'll happen to you a week down the road.

Habits are the building blocks of everything. Or almost everything. A giant chunk of the misfortunes, boons, setbacks, and strokes of golden luck you've experienced in your life were brought about through your habits. Though you may not realize it, your habits have been quietly, steadily laying down the foundation for your very existence. Whether that existence is one you dance through merrily or slog past is determined by what kind of habits you choose to adopt.

Which is where this book comes in. The chapters that follow will introduce you to a total of 144 innovative habits and 36 additional ones, included as a token of appreciation for purchasing this book. These are not manuals on rocket science or quantum phenomena for you to decipher. These are simple, easy-to-implement tools you can use in your life to see quick results and allow the compounding effect of these habits to work its magic. Think of each habit as a little spell to make a small portion of your life go your way. Put many such spells together, continue doing them every day, and what do you get?

A better life.

So, even if you're one of those people who never found John Lennon's quote particularly inspiring or motivating, then read on. You'll find that the information to follow will suit your tastes far better. All 180 habits have been divided into essential themes, each theme addressing a particular domain of your life. There's no need for you to read these themes in the correct order. In fact, there really is no order at all for this book. If you feel that one specific area of your life needs more improvement than the others, by all means, go through that theme first and give it closer attention. Whether it's mental well-being, financial stability, physical fitness, or even just learning to improve your social relationships, this book is a toolbox to help you improve your life.

Just remember one thing: implementing the habits is what will drive forces forward in your life, and only you can do it.

With that being said, you are now ready to kickstart your new journey! If a long journey starts with a single step, doesn't that mean a brand-new life can begin with a single new habit?

That's how fundamental transformation takes place.

One step at a time.

TIME

Optimize your time to be productive, organized,
and create space for what truly matters.

1
Morning Routines

Starting the day with clarity and energy

PLANNING

Review Your Planning at Least Twice

DAILY   **10 MIN**

In the morning every day, review your plans, meetings, and deadlines in your diary—not only for today but also for tomorrow.

Including both days in this simple daily habit allows you to gather your thoughts twice, enabling you to refine your ideas before executing them.

1. A first time, a day ahead, allows enough time to create a first point of view and gauge a potential approach.
2. One more time, on the actual day of the event, allows you to refine your strategy and ensure better execution.

This dual-perspective planning method gives you the mental space to prepare more effectively. Over time, this method helps you build a buffer between you and the potential stress associated with the planned events. It also enables you to take a step back, be more reflective and confident, which will become apparent to others and lead to a better start to the day.

To make it a regular habit, link it to something you already do, such as during breakfast or on the way to work. Each time you do this, make sure to write down any thoughts to integrate ideas you gather along the way.

2

Morning Routines

Starting the day with clarity and energy

PRODUCTIVITY

Find Your Golden Window

📅 **DAILY**   🕐 **2 HOURS**

Your Highest-Energy Window, or *Golden Window*, is that cherished 1- to 2-hour period in your day when your focus and creativity are at their peak. To find your window, remain keenly aware of yourself over two or three weeks and determine when you are at your sharpest. This is a moment in your day when your brain is in its best possible condition for deep thinking, concentration, and focus—and when your productivity is maximized.

Most people find their Golden Windows in the morning when the mind and body are most receptive and rested.

To discover yours:

For two to three weeks, log your energy daily, rating your mental energy on a scale from 1 to 10 every few hours. Make note of the types of activities your brain is most keen to engage in, and those it feels the least ready to tackle.

Try to base this assessment on the activities you most often engage in, such as strategic thinking, creative work, answering emails, etc.

At the end of the experiment, identify your "Golden Window". This becomes your most valuable time block for creativity, problem-solving, strategy, and high-impact work.

The compounding effect of this habit is pretty obvious, as being efficient on essential matters will ensure you optimize the related results.

It's not about doing more; it's about doing what matters most efficiently.

3

Morning Routines
Starting the day with clarity and energy

RECHARGING

Indulge in Calming Rituals of Your Choice

📅 **DAILY**   🕐 **30 MINS**

Do not think of this as an occasional luxury or a waste of time. Every message you send to your body and mind shapes your day, particularly those you send in the morning. Allow yourself 30 minutes daily to detach from work or other stresses in your life, and make this moment mindful.

Connect your ritual with your senses––such as stretching with music and burning oil, or enjoying a hot drink in a quiet space, feeling the fresh air and the sun on your skin.

Whatever it will be, plan it methodically so its logistics do not become part of the ritual, and that the moment is carefully crafted.

What is essential is to create a moment that is entirely yours for you to feel present. Being at the center stage of this moment will build mental strength, control, and emotional clarity.

Remember, setting the scene for your day helps your mind and body to tune in and reminds you that you matter before the world asks anything of you.

4
Prioritization
Focusing on what truly matters

PLANNING

Focus on What Truly Matters

📅 **DAILY**   🕐 **10 MIN**

Each week, dedicate 15 minutes to using the Eisenhower Matrix to review the importance and urgency of the scheduled projects and tasks.

A famous quote from former U.S. President Dwight D. Eisenhower inspired this matrix:

"What is important is seldom urgent, and what is urgent is seldom important."

The matrix helps you see what truly deserves your attention, what should be scheduled, what should be delegated, and what should be ignored.

	Urgent	Not Urgent
Important	Do it now	Schedule it
Not Important	Delegate it	Eliminate it

Once your priorities are clear, reflect them in your planner, starting with your overarching goals and working backward to plan what you need to do or get organized to achieve them.

Your planning must be healthily balanced. You should feel like you're on top of things, rather than in a race against the clock.

5
Prioritization
Focusing on what truly matters

PRODUCTIVITY

Budget Your Time for Projects

📅 **WEEKLY**   🕐 **20 MIN**

An efficient way to stay focused and avoid being overwhelmed is to assign a specific time limit to the things you need to do.

If the project has a large scope, break it down into key milestones. Allocate a balanced number of hours between being realistic and efficient. Breakdown this time across the different milestones throughout a given day or week.

The allocation for a single task can be as simple as "Write report—45 minutes" or "Client research—30 minutes."

To keep this system efficient, these tasks must be treated like appointments, so move on when the time is up, even if everything is not perfect.

This method really forces you to become more efficient over time, avoid perfectionism, and spend 80% of your day on low-priority / low-impact matters.

You will also improve your budgeting skills, making the entire prioritization system even more efficient.

6
Prioritization
Focusing on what truly matters

RECHARGING

Treat Your Personal Time as Your Professional Time

WEEKLY   **15 MIN**

Block time for yourself!

It is so easy to find excuses to get more work done. Still, the reality is that work can be endless—particularly when you are passionate or when it involves stressful factors, such as tight deadlines. Energy is a limited resource, so it is vital to allocate downtime and recharge.

Your calendar needs to reflect your personal priorities— such as sports or workout sessions, time for family and friends, and "me" time. Treat these moments with the same respect as business meetings, which you would not cancel or ignore on a whim.

Just because you work during weekends and holidays does not mean you will be perceived as hard-working. In most professional environments, others will likely find that you aren't organized enough and that your sense of priorities is not strong enough.

If you lead a team, you will set the culture and example for your team, so make sure to lead by example and respect others' privacy as well. The positive impact on people's culture and the respect you will receive in exchange are well worth the effort.

This method will help you set boundaries and avoid burnout.

7

Evening Wind Down

Creating closure and restful transitions

PLANNING

First, Trust What You Want to Achieve

📅 **WEEKLY**　　🕒 **5 MIN**

Research shows that intensely visualizing a future scenario for a prolonged period triggers neurological changes in the brain, causing it to perceive the event as if it has already occurred. This can bias the brain for a positive outcome, for example.

To be successful, you must first think you will be successful. This method emphasizes rehearsing a positive future outcome and primes your brain to make it accurate.

1. Take out a journal and write a one-page note about tomorrow's key events.
2. Detail how they should occur for the day to be successful.
3. At the end of the next day, sit down for a quick reflection session and think about how everything went. What worked? What didn't?

This method helps you approach tomorrow with a positive outlook, prepares you for potential challenges, encourages self-reflection, and enables improvement over time.

8

Evening Wind Down

Creating closure and restful transitions

PRODUCTIVITY

Learn How to Take a Step Back and Strategize

🗓 **DAILY**   🕐 **30 MIN**

If your house starts to feel suffocating, you open the windows and let some fresh air in.

Why would you think your mind works differently?

Clearing out your mental spaces can be hugely helpful if you feel stressed or uneasy about an impending challenge or sensitive situation. Taking a step back is very often the most effective option.

Here's how you open your mind's windows and let the breeze in to help lighten you up:

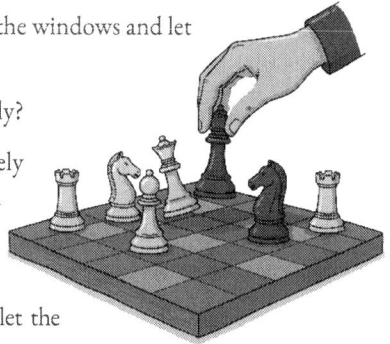

- **First method**: When you feel the urge for an answer to an unpleasant email, draft your response without sending the email and sleep on it until the next morning. It is guaranteed that you will change your email content with wiser words the next day. A two-step approach always ensures a better outcome.
- **Second method**: You may rate on an emotional scale ranging from 1-10 how sensitive tomorrow might be. 10 is a very sensitive day with high stakes. List all possible points of tension you could encounter, note them down, and write down how you will respond to the situations for the best possible outcome. Remain pragmatic in the analysis and in how you intend to respond to the potential challenges.

The two methods above are simple ways to effectively "clear the air" in your mind and better prepare for better outcomes.

9

Evening Wind Down
Creating closure and restful transitions

RECHARGING

Automate Your Sunset Rituals

📅 **DAILY**   🕐 **30 HOURS**

In the world of Well-being, a lot of emphasis is placed on healthy rituals that occur at sunrise. But sending signals to your mind that the day is ending and some personal time is about to start is equally important. Accompanying this moment with recognizable patterns and ideally automating them wherever possible makes it even more efficient.

This technique helps you end your day on a positive note. It is built around Zapier to automate restful routines, ensuring a mindful transition to the evening.

Here are three ways you can use to automate your ritual:

1. **Oil Scent Diffusion**: If you have a smart diffuser, such as those from *Aera* or *Vitruvi*, you can automate it with *Zapier* to release a specific blend of relaxing essential oil scents at a specific time, transiting from the end of your working day to a well-deserved free time by automating the release of lavender and sandalwood for example.

2. **Light Transitioning**: If you have a smart lighting system, you can program *Zapier* to begin dimming lights gently during the last hour of work. Open the light-controlling app, pair it with *Zapier,* and follow the instructions. This subtle change of light invites you into a restful state without you even realizing it, and is excellent for relieving eye stress.

3. **Sound Bath**: Nature is known for its therapeutic qualities, and simulating the sounds of nature in your office can be a great way to conclude a draining day. You can program *Zapier* to play with the sound of gentle rain, lapping waves, or a mixture of forest animals to scrub your mind clean of worries and ensure you don't carry your work home with you. Pair your *Zapier* app with your office speakers, then choose the correct track on Spotify or any other music app. Set the right trigger time on *Zapier*, and you're ready!

10
Time Blocking
Structuring your day intentionally

PLANNING

Create a "Weekly Flow Map" with Daily Themes

📅 WEEKLY 🕐 10 MIN

Life is all about flow. If you can find yours, you'll be cruising your way to success in no time.

To find your flow, organize your week like one glorious tango. Devote each day to a specific mood, using a regular rhythm.

Below, a sample planner has been created to help you out:

1. Monday (Strategic) – Time to strategize! Focus on creativity and strategic thinking today. You may also involve relevant team members.
2. Tuesday (Delegation) – Once your strategies have been established, it could be the right day to delegate this strategy. Choose the right person to delegate to and share clear goals and deadlines.
3. Wednesday (Connection) - This is your people's day. Use it for networking, calls, and collaborations.
4. Thursday (Delivery) - Time for your efforts to pay off. Use this day to execute all plans and strategies. This is more of a task-focused day.
5. Friday (Reflection) - How'd the week go? What could you have done better? Friday is for learning, empathy, and striving to do even better next time.

Remember: such planning ensures having the right mindset at the right time to allow for undivided attention, thus improving focus. Build the week to match a suitable rhythm for you.

11

Time Blocking

Structuring your day intentionally

PRODUCTIVITY

Benefit Fully from Your Golden Window

DAILY   **2 HOURS**

Now that you've identified your Golden Window--the time of day when your focus is sharpest and creativity flows most freely--it's time to make the best use of it and care for it.

Prioritize your most essential and high-impact activities, those that require undistracted time. Choose activities requiring creativity, strategy, problem-solving, or emotional understanding--those that are usually harder to process.

During this time, it is recommended to remove any possible distractions, such as your phone and unnecessary browser tabs. Be sure to let others know you're unavailable by blocking the two hours off in your calendar, for example.

Do not check or answer messages and emails. They are easy to process, which is often why most people do this first thing in the morning--though this is a bad practice. They can be easily done in the early afternoon or at the end of the day, when the brain and mental energy usually dip.

To summarize, once you've found this window, do the following to make the most of it:

- Block it on your calendar with recurring notices.
- Tell your team not to disturb you during that timeframe.
- Switch off your phone and other electronic devices.
- Minimize outside distractions.
- Dive deep into your work's most strategic, challenging, and creative aspects.

Extra tip: You may also choose a dedicated space to spend this 2-hour window at and pair it with a ritual, such as playing instrumental music, brewing coffee, or brewing tea.

See the results unfold!

12

Time Blocking

Structuring your day intentionally

RECHARGING

Gamify Goals to Achieve Them

📅 **WEEKLY**   🕐 **30 MIN**

Tricking your mind is often the most efficient way to overcome the hardship of tasks that need to be performed.

An innovative way to set goals in a fun way is to imagine next week as a movie or game with a central theme, objectives, and side quests.

Every Sunday, update your personal dashboard by:

MISSION
MORE SALES
Agent $007

- Deciding on one primary mission to become your top goal for the week.
- Choose a codename, for example, "Operation Finish That Deck" or "Mission Find New Leads".
- Underneath, add two or three side quests relating to the same theme.
- Consider the people involved as movie or game characters and write down their roles.

Planning and executing do not always have to be boring or serious. Gamifying helps add fun and playfulness to things you would have regarded as boring or repetitive.

13

Delegation & Saying No

Freeing space and mental load

PLANNING

Design Your "Let-Go Board"

📅 **DAILY**   🕐 **10 MIN**

Trying to handle everything yourself will drive you––or everyone else around you––insane. You need to learn to delegate tasks, but this is easier said than done.

The *Let-Go Board* is ideal for facilitating effective delegation. Preferably on a wallboard, create a visual space where every delegated task, written on a Post-it, moves across five stages. The more creative and visually impactful your board is, the more engaging and fun it will be!

A few ideas include using color-coded sticky notes, painted wooden blocks for each task or assignee, or even a magnetized whiteboard with differently shaped magnets.

The general board layout will be similar to this:

- **Stage 1: Strategic thinking** – decide who is the best-placed person to achieve a specific task.
- **Stage 2: Handover** – The task has been delegated to the owner with clear instructions. Depending on your board, this could mean posting colored sticky notes with someone's name and another with the task, or a more creative adaptation to the same concept.
- **Stage 3: Trust Mode** – You consciously let go and only review the milestones, avoiding micromanagement. This step involves no action until the delegated task and person picked move to the next stage.
- **Stage 4: Supporting Follow-Up** – During that pre-defined period, you stay updated at regular intervals––but only for support, not to control.
- **Stage 5: Victory** – Time for the final review. If the task was completed without your interference, move them into a 6th box to remind you that you did a good job. If the task wasn't completed as you wished, move the sticky note back to Stage 4.

Bonus: You can add emojis to make the delegation process fun and easier to manage.

14

Delegation & Saying No

Freeing space and mental load

PRODUCTIVITY

Tag Incoming Tasks and Duties

🗓 **DAILY**   🕐 **10 MIN**

The *Tag System* turns work into a fun game. All you need to do is write down and tag each incoming task with an emoji that describes how it makes you feel. For example:

💧   Urgent & energizing

💤   Draining

💬   Strategic

💼   Could someone else carry this?

Block time over two days per week to strategize by reviewing the 💬 tasks. Such thinking sessions cannot be delegated, but the presence of others may be needed.

Daily, in the early afternoon, address the 💤 tasks by completing, negotiating, or assigning them. Similarly, find the most suitable person for the tasks.

Taking care of strategic tasks and delegating what can be delegated will free up negative emotions and prepare you better for the 💧 functions with all your energy, passion, and focus.

The Tag System enables us to categorize and process tasks effectively, thereby reducing the emotional burden.

With a lighter heart, you're ready to face the day with high spirits, greater efficiency, and a clear mind.

15

Delegation & Saying No

Freeing space and mental load

RECHARGING

Delegation Dice

📅 **DAILY**   🕐 **1 MIN**

Often, low-impact decisions are the first cause of creating overwhelming feelings. They also generally reduce focus on the important ones.

This method helps you deal with these low-impact decisions and relieves you from caring too much about them.

To start, create your own unique delegation dice by purchasing a physical one online, using a DIY template to create one, or downloading an app. Remember to make your delegation dice fun by customizing the faces with smileys, for example, and give each side a personalized, funky touch!

Once this is done––and whenever a low-impact decision comes your way––roll the dice to decide your next course of action.

The options are:

- Delegate it
- Say no
- Do it later
- Ask for help
- Simplify it
- Breathe and roll again

Leaving it all to the dice lightens the seriousness of situations you tend to create for yourself and removes pressure––all in a fun, game-like manner!

This method should only target low-impact decisions, of course.

16
Optimization
Doing more with less effort

PLANNING

Organize Your Calendar to Look Like Tetris

🗓️ **WEEKLY**   🕐 **15 MIN**

Are you too young to know Tetris, or do you feel nostalgic at the thought of it?

Every week, on Friday, for example, you rearrange your calendar as if you were playing Tetris to help maximize time efficiency.

1. **Color-coding**: Use vibrant colors to categorize your tasks by theme, making them look like Tetris blocks!
2. **Combo Tasks**: Level up the game with combos! Organize similar tasks together so that time spent on specific days is dedicated to a particular theme, which in turn helps you concentrate on that theme.
3. **Strategic/Rush Mode**: Ensure tasks are organized according to the mental effort required. For example, some strategic days should be reserved for strategic meetings or financial reviews only.

A Tetris-themed calendar turns time optimization into a fun and exciting process. It helps you take a strategic look at your time allocation, allowing for greater focus and energy, and ensuring that both the quality and quantity of your output increase.

17

Optimization

Doing more with less effort

PRODUCTIVITY

The Two-Tap System

📅 **DAILY**   🕐 **2 MIN**

Overthinking rarely helps, even in the best of circumstances. More often, it leads to delays and being overwhelmed.

Use the *Two-Tap System* to eliminate this problem once and for all.

The *Two-Tap System* operates according to the following rules:

- **First Tap**: When a new task appears, evaluate whether it can be dealt with in under 2 minutes. If yes, complete the task immediately. If not, move to the Second Tap. This method is inspired by David Allen, an American productivity consultant and author of *Getting Things Done*.
- **Second Tap**: For longer tasks, quickly decide how they should be completed––whether by rescheduling, delegation, or simply disregarding them (not all tasks deserve your attention!). Remember—the point is to save time, improve your productivity, and avoid getting bogged down in details. Swiftly decide without overthinking and then move on to the next task.

The *Two-Tap System* is a highly efficient way to handle tasks and avoid wasting time.

The system provides a framework for decision-making, prevents overthinking, and draws you into tasks that do not warrant your time.

18
Optimization
Doing more with less effort

RECHARGING

Double Up to Optimize Effects

📅 **DAILY**   🕐 **10 MIN**

Looking at ways to become truly productive? Time to take advantage of the *Double-Up Effect*!

The "*Double-up Effect*" entails precisely what its name suggests: using two beneficial activities in tandem to save time and increase productivity.

Here are a few examples:

1. **Household Activities x Educational Content**: The more you learn, the more you grow. Utilize your time dedicated to household activities, such as cleaning or cooking, to enhance your technical or business knowledge by listening to informative podcasts and implementing the lessons learned.
2. **Phone Calls x Walking Breaks**: Dedicate a portion of your day to taking work outdoors. When connecting with clients or colleagues over scheduled calls, consider incorporating refreshing activities, such as walking or bicycling, into your routine. The call will ensure your work progresses, whereas the walk will help stimulate your body.
3. **Networking x Golf**: Be innovative and organize your next networking or client event around a sports activity that helps you connect and exercise. Networking events in the business world can be either very boring or very unhealthy, with a lot of drinking and partying. With wellness becoming a stronger theme, connecting around a sports activity, such as golf, pickleball, or even pétanque, is a great way to combine the best of both worlds.

Time is the most valuable currency of all, and your ability to use it smartly determines your level of success. The *Double-Up Effect* is a great way to boost your productivity.

19

Deep Work
Techniques for focused work

PLANNING

Use Focus Planning Cards

📅 **DAILY**   🕐 **5 MIN**

The *Focus Planning Card* can be an effective method for handling more complex tasks. This method helps you define your goal, outline the first steps, and identify tasks to support deep-focused work.

Here's how you use it:

- Cut out three equal, card-shaped rectangles from a piece of paper.
- Place one card horizontally in the center.
- Staple the other two cards vertically from the center card's opposite ends.
- The center card is your task. The remaining two hanging from its ends are the outcome (on the right) and the first step (on the left).
- Fill in the cards, starting with the desired outcome, then the task list in the middle, and finishing with the first step.
- Get to work!

Although it may sound overly simplistic, the Focus Card improves strategic thinking and productivity in a more tactile and innovative way.

20

Deep Work
Techniques for focused work

PRODUCTIVITY

Optimize Time-Efficiency with the Pomodoro Technique

🗓️ **DAILY**   🕐 **25 MIN**

The *Pomodoro Technique* is a productivity hack designed by the Italian productivity consultant Francesco Cirillo in the late 1980s. He devised the technique while he was a university student, facing the same struggle that has been eternally haunting students since the dawn of time: the inability to maintain focus while studying.

Determined to increase his productivity, Francesco used a tomato-shaped (Pomodoro) kitchen timer to break down his studying sessions into deep-focused work segments, and thus the famous *Pomodoro technique* was born.

Here's how you use it:

1. Pick a task that needs to be completed.
2. Set a timer for 25 minutes.
3. Begin working on that task, and keep your focus on it until the timer buzzes. Keep your focus.
4. After the 25 minutes are up, take a 5-minute short break to recover from your productivity sprint. The break should be as deep as your focus on your task: listen to some music, have a good drink, or take a brief stretch break.
5. Repeat the cycle until you've completed four Pomodoros (2 hours). Then, take a longer break of 30 minutes, preparing yourself to begin another cycle or to move on to new deep-focused work.

Why is the *Pomodoro Technique* so effective? Simple: for the same reason a sprinter is faster than a marathon runner. It's about deep intensity intervals rather than maintaining a long, exhausting pace.

21

Deep Work
Techniques for focused work

RECHARGING

Reset Your Brain with the Eyes, Air, Away Method

📅 **DAILY**   🕒 **5 MIN**

Sometimes, it can all be a bit too much: your computer's harsh glow, that uncomfortably hard office chair beneath you, and the fan's slow, infuriating drone, all conspiring to turn your brain into mush until you can get no more work done.

The *Eyes, Air, and Away method* is scientifically backed and is most effective in preventing brain overheating. Use it regularly to keep your mind functioning at its best and your eyesight from deteriorating, so your productivity and health don't decline during long working hours.

Here is what the *Eyes, Air, and Away method* stands for and how to implement it:

- **E - Eyes**: Every 20 minutes, look away from your monitor at another object that's at least 20 feet away. Do this for 20 seconds.
- **A - Air**: Step outdoors into fresh air. Remain there for at least 5 minutes, breathing deeply and consciously.
- **A - Away**: It's easy to get away physically, but mental distance is the real challenge. During your Eyes, Air and Away break, don't allow yourself to think about anything work-related, no matter how pressing. Think of this period as recharging time for your brain.

Eyes, Air, and Away is a simple yet effective method, particularly for workaholics who grind away endless hours but struggle with decreasing productivity over time. This quick hack allows you to reset your focus levels and avoid overheating.

Regular eye breaks help limit eye strain, allowing you to blink more frequently and thereby preventing dryness and vision blurriness. Similarly, stepping outdoors regulates your circadian cycle, which in turn boosts your mood and energy levels.

22
Efficiency Tools
Using calendars, task managers, and automation

PLANNING

Use AI to Triage Your To-Do List

📅 **WEEKLY**   🕐 **5 MIN**

Always dreamed of having an assistant? Why wait? Use a virtual one!

Delegating to others is not always possible, and AI can be a fantastic tool for streamlining work. Use these newly developed tools to help you tackle tasks efficiently.

Checklist

☑ **Low Priority**
☑ **Medium Priority**
☑ **High Priority**

A properly phrased prompt asking *ChatGPT* to sort and prioritize your to-do list, along with time estimates, can be a powerful way to organize yourself and save time. It'll also free up your schedule, allowing you to accomplish even more.

Here's a sample prompt you can give *ChatGPT* to turn your week into an efficient one:

Optimize my weekly to-do list by sorting and grouping tasks into relevant categories, prioritizing them based on urgency and importance, and estimating the time needed to complete each task. Suggest any opportunities for batching similar tasks to improve efficiency and recommend the best way to tackle them for maximum productivity.

Try it!

23
Efficiency Tools
Using calendars, task managers, and automation

PRODUCTIVITY

Automate Recurring Tasks Using Technology

📅 **DAILY**   🕐 **1 HOUR**

Time is your business's vital life force. The more of it you have, the more effective it will be.

Use the *Zapier* app to automate repetitive workflows and free yourself up for more significant, value-driven tasks.

Zapier is an automation tool that connects your apps, enabling them to work together seamlessly without requiring any coding and with minimal user input.

Here are a few examples of how you can use *Zapier* to boost productivity:

1. **Optimize Team Management**: Every time a new task is created on Asana (project management app), *Zapier* automatically creates a relevant event on the calendar outlining the task details and completion deadline before sending a Slack notification (team messaging and collaboration platform) to the assigned team member, thereby keeping everyone aligned.

2. **Follow-up Checks**: Each time an email with an attachment is received, the file is automatically downloaded to *Google Drive*, and the recipient is notified on Slack to ensure efficiency in communication.

3. **Content Creation**: Whenever a new company blog is published, *Zapier* automatically tweets the link, uploads the content to the respective *LinkedIn* page, and sends an email to the relevant subscriber list, ensuring maximum content visibility with minimal effort.

Once the system is in place, it can easily save hours of work. If you feel intimidated by learning *Zapier*, consider hiring a Zapier Engineer on *Fiverr* to help you set things up.

24

Efficiency Tools

Using calendars, task managers, and automation

RECHARGING

Become Emotionally Aware

📅 **DAILY**   🕐 **5 MIN**

Anaïs Nin, a French-Cuban-American writer, once said: "We don't see the world as it is; we see the world as we are."

This little pearl of wisdom holds even in the professional sphere. Stability of mind and mood is essential for clear interaction with the world, and being aware of your state helps you navigate these interactions in the best possible way.

Apps like *Daylio* and *Reflectly* are excellent tools for managing your inner world and gaining a deeper understanding of your behaviors.

Here are some of the features they offer:

1. **Mood Tracking**: By inputting your emotional state and how it varies throughout the day, the app can deduce your mood patterns and provide valuable insights, helping you identify triggers.
2. **Mood Rating**: The app enables you to rate your overall mood each day and provides personalized suggestions to enhance your well-being.
3. **Mood Alerts**: The app also notifies you when it detects low mood levels for an unusually long duration. Such alerts can help you quickly return to your baseline, ensuring you don't approach work with a negative or limiting mindset.

Tracking your mood throughout the day and remaining aware of the most common emotions you experience means knowing yourself, which will set you up for success. You'll know when to make critical decisions and when to hold back.

FINANCE

Grow financial wealth to unlock freedom, stability,
and future possibilities.

25

Budgeting & Tracking

Awareness of inflow and outflow

EARNING / SPENDING

Maintain a Personal Profit & Loss Statement

📅 **WEEKLY**　　🕐 **30 MIN**

Manage personal finance like company finance. Handling earnings wisely enables the compounding effect, allowing for substantial capital growth over time.

Record your earnings and expenses at the end of each week, usually by reviewing your bank or credit card statements. Don't leave anything out, including expenses such as food, rent, and movie tickets. Expenses should be categorized to allow you to track the performance of cost centers.

At the end of the month, sit down for a personal "Profit & Loss" review with yourself. Write down your monthly income minus taxes in Excel, then list your cost categories and the corresponding total for each category. The bottom line is your savings.

Reserve the following columns for the following month's performances and alternate with a variance column to track movements in earnings and costs, month after month.

From there, you can calculate your daily savings (monthly savings divided by the number of days in the month) or your savings rate (as a percentage: monthly savings divided by your after-tax income). It provides you with simple KPIs (Key Performance Indicators) to help you outperform daily and build better expense habits.

A relevant example is removing the daily habit of buying a $3 coffee, which saves you $1,095 annually.

Do not lower your lifestyle, but do not underestimate the compounding effect either.

26

Budgeting & Tracking

Awareness of inflow and outflow

INVESTING

Match Purchases with a Proportional Investment

📅 **SET UP ONCE**   🕐 **1 HOUR**

This method allows you to enjoy purchases while balancing them with a proportional saving, thereby removing the guilt associated with making purchases and keeping your investment in mind.

The system is simple:

Every time you make a non-essential purchase, deposit 10% of its value into an investment account.

That's it. That's the system, and it's very effective due to its two-fold benefits: you continue to enjoy what you enjoy and save every time you do. This habit does not have a restrictive component, so to speak.

Even better. This habit can be automated with Apps like *Acorn*, ensuring some money is automatically invested whenever you have expenses. It can also be invested in specific asset classes, such as Bitcoin and others.

Learning to enjoy today while saving every time you do naturally builds balanced finances.

Budgeting & Tracking

Awareness of inflow and outflow

MINDSET/IMPACT

Write Your Money Principles

📅 **MONTHLY**　　🕐 **15 MIN**

Today, increasing evidence supports the claim that our thoughts can influence reality. Because change comes from within, writing your money principles and evolving them over time changes your relationship with money at the pace of your discovery of finance.

The method can be applied as follows:

1. **Awareness**: To shed limiting beliefs, you must first be aware of them. In a journal, write down what you truly believe about money principles.
2. **Change/Remove Beliefs**: Every month, change or remove beliefs that need to be removed and explain why it was necessary.
3. **Add New Belief**: Every month, take a careful look at your monthly finances, including how you spend, earn, and invest your money. Write any new beliefs that come to mind. From there, you have new money principles.

Approaching your relationship with money by journaling your beliefs will solidify your principles and empower you to implement effective practices.

28

Emergency Fund

Security and peace of mind

EARNING/SPENDING

Dedicate One Skill to One Bill

📅 **DAILY**   🕐 **1 HOUR**

Also known as a side hustle and, quite frankly, a principle embodying the spirit of entrepreneurship in itself, the concept is that one of your recurring bills will be paid with an additional income coming from an activity of your choice.

You must create a new income stream to eliminate one of your recurring expenses, which you will pick by yourself. Activities can broadly vary based on where you live, your skills, and your preferences:

It could, for example, be freelancing as a graphic designer or trimming someone's lawn. You can find relevant freelancing opportunities on platforms like *Fiverr* and *Upwork*, whereas jobs like lawn trimming can come from retired persons in your neighborhood.

Be creative. If you aren't or do not have enough inspiration, why not ask an AI bot for suggestions?

This habit helps you grow your entrepreneurship spirit and increase savings without reducing costs.

29

Emergency Fund

Security and peace of mind

INVESTING

Invest the Round-Ups

DAILY   **AUTOMATIC**

The more effortless and fun the investment process is, the more consistent the investment will be.

Investing spare change from everyday purchases is a great way to contribute to your investment portfolio without negatively affecting your lifestyle.

Spare change investment consists of rounding up your bill and investing the difference.

For example, a coffee costing $2.60 would be considered a $3 purchase, with $0.4 being invested.

Automating the process entirely makes it easier, and several apps are available, depending on your location.

Acorn is available in the US and can assist you with this, but there are several other options on the market.

With *Acorn*, you can choose your risk level and even set specific savings goals; the app will then invest in an appropriate portfolio for you.

To make the process even more fun, you can choose a creative, attention-grabbing name for your fund, such as the "Stress-Free Vault", etc. This name contributes to your fund's emotional connection and helps you achieve your goal.

Using a round-up investing method like this makes saving easy.

30

Emergency Fund

Security and peace of mind

MINDSET / IMPACT

Audit Your Personal Liquidity Level

YEARLY   **1 HOUR**

Companies assess their liquidity level through their balance sheets. Have you ever done this for your personal finances? What if you need emergency money? Are you prepared?

In the event of an emergency, you may need to access funds quickly. Just like a company, assessing your liquidity level helps you understand how liquid your personal assets are and, in general, enables you to maintain a reasonable liquidity level in your investment.

Financial Asset Liquidity can be divided into four categories and easily listed in *Excel*, as below:

1. **Very Liquid**: The assets are accessible instantly. This is generally cash at the bank.
2. **Liquid**: These assets take two to three days to access. They are generally funds or other relatively liquid investments.
3. **Not So Liquid**: These assets can take three days to a month to liquidate. It could be physical assets, such as a car or other sellable items.
4. **Illiquid**: These assets take more than a month to access. A good example of this type of asset is a house or an apartment.

Once you know the liquidity level of your assets, you can establish a healthy balance to ensure you are not fully invested in illiquid assets.

Conducting a monthly liquidity audit like this one helps you anticipate any unexpected challenges.

31

Smart Spending

Needs vs wants, conscious consumerism

EARNING/SPENDING

Spend Money on What Makes You Truly Happy

📅 **WEEKLY**　🕐 **10 MIN**

The modern age of technology bombards us with advertisements on every occasion. As a result, many of our actions cannot truly be said to be our own but are a product of subtle brainwashing and a culture of overconsumption.

The method raises awareness of how you *spend money* by analyzing purchases based on the joy your expenses bring. It works as follows:

- Track down all purchases in a defined period, categorizing purchases by theme (e.g., food, travel, etc.)
- Rate each purchase on a Joy Scale ranging from 1 to 10, with 1 representing little to no satisfaction and 10 indicating extreme satisfaction.
- Divide the purchasing prices of the different expenses by that number to get the *Cost per Joy*.
- Analyze results on the *Costs per Joy* basis instead of the actual purchasing costs and decide which one is worth keeping and which one could be reduced or, even better, discontinued completely.

Implementing this habit helps you become a conscious consumer who gets better value for their money.

Being aware of the actual value of your expenses allows you to focus on purchases that provide genuine satisfaction and reduce less satisfactory expenses, thereby increasing your savings and overall satisfaction with the money spent.

32

Smart Spending

Needs vs wants, conscious consumerism

INVESTING

Invest in Expenses Supporting Your Lifestyle

📅 **DAILY**　　🕐 **10 MIN**

This method is another efficient way to help you consume more wisely and save money in proportion to your spending.

The rule is simple: invest a defined portion of your expenses into a company-associated stock each time you purchase a non-essential item.

For example, when buying running shoes, consider investing 10% of the cost in a reputable fitness brand. Or, if you're going on a trip, invest 10% of the total cost in your favorite airline or hotel brands.

Over time, this micro-investing behavior builds awareness of your spending habits while gradually growing a portfolio that reflects your lifestyle.

This habit can connect purchases with ownership and purpose, thereby stimulating investments without effort.

It is also innovative because an investment portfolio is usually made based on income, rather than expenses.

33

Smart Spending

Needs vs wants, conscious consumerism

MINDSET/IMPACT

Upgrade Purchases Once to Never Regret

📅 **YEARLY**   🕐 **1 HOUR**

Spending more does not always mean spending stupidly, as long as the quality of a product better sustains the test of time––meaning lower likelihood of replacement and more money saved.

This method allows you to save costs by listing all items frequently replaced by nature––such as belts, bags, shoes, etc. Consider upgrading to higher-quality alternatives for longer-term savings.

List the usual costs of all these items and how often you replace them. Based on these numbers, deduct a yearly cost.

For example:

Suppose you choose a belt costing you 20$. However, the belt is made of synthetic leather and looks worn out after three months, meaning you'll need to replace it four times a year. The yearly cost is $80.

Wouldn't a better belt, even three times more expensive, made of genuine leather, and which you may only need to replace once a year, have been a better purchasing choice?

Mathematically, it would have.

Engaging in such assessments allows you to spend more wisely, save money over time, and even purchase better brands and higher-quality products.

34

Future Success

Simple, long-term investing strategies

EARNING/SPENDING

One-Month Business Tester

QUARTERLY   **30 DAYS**

Life doesn't wait for anyone, and neither should you! The greatest businesses often began as small-scale business ideas. Don't let your limited finances or risk-averse nature stop you from pursuing your entrepreneurial dreams.

Use the *One-Month Business Tester* habit to explore this world without too much risk.

The Business Tester method requires that you dip your toes into the business pond once every three months.

The goal is to develop a low-cost, low-risk business idea and refine it over 30 days. See how you perform. Measure your profit and note down the obstacles you encounter.

At the end of the 30 days, you can decide whether to continue with your project, scale it up, or drop it altogether.

If you decide to drop it, you must pick up another business idea within three months and give it a 30-day trial run once again.

What you choose to work on is entirely your choice, making the habit fun and engaging.

Here are some possible tester ideas to get your creative juices flowing:

- Running a small-scale confectionery e-store from home.
- Creating a specialized e-commerce store
- Launching a print-on-demand product.

The *One-Month Business Tester* habit accustoms you to the entrepreneurial world without significant risk or stress exposure.

It's the perfect way for working professionals or stay-at-home moms with limited time who are looking to scale their income.

35

Future Success

Simple, long-term investing strategies

INVESTING

Scout for Micro-Investment in New Trends

📅 **MONTHLY**   🕐 **4 HOURS**

The most significant opportunities in life don't call for investing in them, so staying aware and ready for them is essential.

Every month, select an emerging theme, conduct light research on it, read up on the latest trends, and highlight anything that sparks your interest.

Invest a small amount ($10–$50) in one company or product related to that theme, then repeat the process the following month, keeping the recurring investment intentionally light.

The theme could be anything emerging enough that draws your interest, from a niche wellness brand to a new AI tool gaining popularity.

The point is to get involved in research, stay updated with the latest emerging trends, and enjoy the learning process.

You can even keep a "Trendfolio" journal where you note down all items of interest and keep tabs on them.

Following this habit consistently helps you stay aware and informed in a rapidly evolving world, boosting your chances of spotting the next big thing as it emerges.

36

Future Success

Simple, long-term investing strategies

MINDSET / IMPACT

Compete Around Passive Income with Your Friends

📅 **MONTHLY**   🕐 **2 HOURS**

We tend to take examples from the people surrounding us naturally. So, to be exemplary, you'd better have exemplary company around you.

This habit is your gateway to fostering connections with ambitious, like-minded people.

The goal is simple: connect with friends every month to review entrepreneurial initiatives that you are all engaged in.

Write down pointers for each other, giving special attention to the obstacles faced and the advantages gained. Keep the tone light-hearted and encouraging.

Score each person after they present their ideas and results. Maintain competitiveness across key performance indicators, including revenue, profit, and social impact.

The goal is to create a community that fosters and supports ambition, career success, and entrepreneurship.

Speaking with people trying out different avenues removes the excess fear associated with experimentation and pushes you to try harder.

It's a great way to turn your solo journey into a group exploration, where you can draw on others' experiences when needed and even get help to grow your business.

37

Income Diversification

Side hustles, passive income

EARNING/SPENDING

Invest in Yourself

📅 **MONTHLY**   🕐 **5 HOURS**

To find good investment options, start by looking around you.

For every X dollar you invest traditionally, repurpose 10% of that amount in yourself––with that being a mini online course or a distributable digital tool.

The point is to enable you to capitalize on your skills and generate income. If you can stick long enough to anything, you will inevitably be good at it, and success will materialize in some shape or form.

In this case, investing in yourself means investing actively rather than passively in any personal project you choose, which is quite the opposite of traditional investment, where you effectively invest in others.

The advantage of this habit is that it helps you grow in tandem with your investments. It is the foundation for building your skills and confidence while developing recurring income.

38

Income Diversification

Side hustles, passive income

INVESTING

Invest in Royalty Businesses

📅 MONTHLY   🕐 2 DAYS

Financial freedom is nothing without free time, and stimulating our creative spirit, in one way or another, is a great way to develop passive income and reclaim our time.

Each month, conduct some research and choose a platform for which you will create a digital asset. It could be anything, such as:

- Launching an eBook on Amazon
- Creating music to sell on Spotify
- Generating affiliate marketing revenue with a website
- Selling digital arts

The goal is to create without focusing too much on perfection or the odds of success.

Once done, choose a new platform to work on next month and begin adding each of your creative products to a Royalty Portfolio to track the number of orders, customer ratings, and revenue.

One step at a time, you are well on your way to a financially passive future! But the benefits of this habit aren't just financial. It also stimulates your creativity in multiple domains and helps you remain aware of the ins and outs of various digital marketplaces.

39

Income Diversification

Side hustles, passive income

MINDSET/IMPACT

Use Crowdfunding to Leverage Investment

📅 QUARTERLY   🕐 15 DAYS

"Just do it."

That's what the world-famous sports brand *Nike's* slogan says. Just do it. Just take that shot. Just make that jump. See what happens because money always rewards entrepreneurship and courage.

Each quarter, browse e-commerce platforms like *Gumroad* and *Kickstarter* to get an idea of a product you have a realistic chance of launching. Search for products that you can either enhance or better advertise.

It could be anything, from an online trading course, a diet book, a VR chatbot, or even a physical product such as a board game. The choice is yours. Just ensure the idea is both easily achievable and implementable. Keep it low-stakes and have fun.

Channel your creativity, rather than treating it like a commitment. You can even share your ideas with a friend for feedback and improvement.

This habit expands your entrepreneurial reach, potentially giving you access to funds without requiring a large personal investment and increasing your chances of success.

40

Debt Management

Avoiding and reducing toxic debt

EARNING / SPENDING

Use a Side Hustle to Cover Debts

📅 MONTHLY   🕐 2 DAYS

To cover debt, you can either cut a portion of your recurring investments or budget, which often impacts your life, or you can cover it with additional income, which is always preferable.

Lightening debt with a side hustle can do just that and free you up from bad debt and interest faster, avoiding a negative impact on your lifestyle.

This habit requires you to block out an entire weekend every month and dedicate it to income-generating activities.

Find a quick and easy way to earn additional money and use it to cover your debts. Whether you offer tutoring services, sell unused items, or work as a barista is up to you. The point is to ensure that you focus on earning incremental income to cover the monthly value of your debt.

Developing this habit will enable you to make faster progress on your path to freedom, rather than deducting from your regular income stream every month. Even for debts without interest, this habit will help you rid yourself of any obligations, financially and mentally freeing you.

Debt Management

Avoiding and reducing toxic debt

INVESTING

Invest Saving Accruals in Trends Research

📅 **QUARTERLY**   🕐 **90 MIN**

This simple habit will help you grow your financial awareness and keep you better informed when investing your money.

This time savings is accumulated over 3 months before being invested.

For example, dedicate 30 minutes to studying financial trends, data, and news on the first Monday of every month.

At the end of the 3 months, your savings will either be invested in one selected industry or trend through an ETF investment, for example, or used to pay off your debt. The choice will be made based on your investment performance for the past quarter.

This investment strategy enables you to maintain awareness of investment opportunities, make data-driven, intentional decisions, and ensure that your investments are more substantial when made, given the accrual system, effectively giving more weight to your investment decisions and increasing your self-confidence over time.

In the long term, you will have a portfolio of investments in industries you are familiar with, allowing you to refine your strategy.

42

Debt Management

Avoiding and reducing toxic debt

MINDSET/IMPACT

Understand Your Debt Fully

⊞ MONTHLY   🕐 1 HOUR

The actual burden of debt isn't financial, but psychological. The real reason it can be so crippling is because it preys on your mind day and night, filling you with anxiety. As a result, your self-confidence, productivity, and performance suffer, and you're even less likely to pay back that debt.

You can use a data-driven approach to regain control over your debt.

Conduct a monthly debt analysis exercise as a pragmatic and straightforward liability assessment. Note down in a spreadsheet with as much objectivity as possible:

- Total amount owed
- Interest rate
- Minimum payment
- Current balance
- Payment status
- Lending terms & conditions (particularly loan deferment, payment holiday, grace period, loan restructuring, refinancing, etc.)
- Any dedicated income offsetting the debt (rental income, incremental income, etc.)

Think of the numbers and conditions as part of a math problem you must approach with pragmatism.

It will enable you to think strategically about your debt and explore options, such as generating new income and developing backup plans in case of unexpected issues.

Having a pragmatic view of your finances alleviates worries and increases your confidence in your decisions and priorities.

43

Minimalism & Value

Buying for function and joy

EARNING/SPENDING

Control the Types of Purchases You Make

📅 **DAILY**   🕐 **15 MIN**

Your money is yours, meaning you can spend it any way you like. However, most money problems often stem from poor spending habits.

Purchasing assets could be categorized into three types:

1.   Assets that appreciate or generate value over time (e.g., a collection watch)
2.   Assets that serve practical or functional purposes (e.g., furniture)
3.   Assets for status, impression, or identity expression (e.g., designer handbags)

If you want to maximize the efficiency of your spending, don't waste your money trying to impress others. Instead, assess what type of purchases you make each time you make a purchase.

Ask yourself those questions:

- Will the purchased item gain value over time, and is it easy to resell it?
- Can I generate money with it as part of a side business?
- Does this item serve a functional purpose essential to living?
- Does this item improve my life?

If you generally answer 'no' to those questions, reconsider buying.

You could even maintain a "Function First" journal in which you analyze purchases a month after they are made, to see how well they pay off.

Rate each past purchase on a scale of 1-5 based on functionality and "happiness return". Check the average score of all past purchases, and you'll know how impulsively you spend your hard-earned cash.

With this habit, greater self-control and more innovative thought processes will develop, ultimately leading to better savings and better value for the money spent.

44

Minimalism & Value

Buying for function and joy

INVESTING

Spend on What Can Earn You Money

📅 **DAILY**   🕐 **15 MIN**

We all spend some money on non-essential items occasionally, and that's okay. But if you do it too frequently, this habit will help you turn those needless expenses into potential ways to earn money.

The rule is simple: each time you make a non-essential purchase, you must brainstorm at least two ways to monetize that item. For example, a new musical instrument could be used to make *YouTube* videos, or a new car could be rented or operated part-time as an *Uber*.

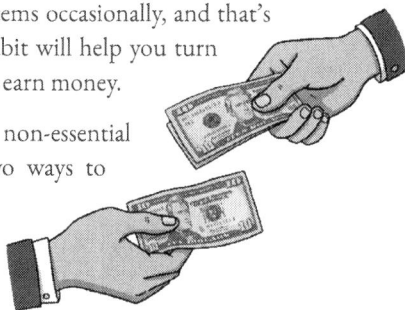

The idea is to be creative, develop side income, and create an entrepreneurial mind, keeping things fun and interesting. Think of out-of-the-box uses and exciting methods to monetize purchases. Even if you cannot earn any income straightaway, having a mindset like this will stimulate hidden opportunities.

And for those purchases that don't seem to have any monetizable aspect, perhaps reconsider whether you really need them or why it is you want them.

45

Minimalism & Value

Buying for function and joy

MINDSET/IMPACT

Step Back to Control Impulsive Purchases

DAILY   **30 HOURS**

We've all been there. You see that flashy new bag or jacket sparkling in a store window, and suddenly, your feet are moving on their own, and your hands are drawing money out of your wallet to spend on an item you'll regret buying the next morning.

If the above story sounds familiar, stepping back before deciding is just what you need, as the habit title suggests.

Next time you see something irresistibly attractive in a shop or an online ad, you have to resist from buying it for the next 30 hours.

During those 30 hours, let yourself decide whether you want it. Help yourself by asking yourself:

- Will I still want this in 30 days?
- What will I use it for?
- Is it better than what I currently own?

If the answer is yes and you are going ahead with your purchase, take the time to look up the item online, consider second-hand, etc.

Giving your impulses time to simmer down will make every purchase thoughtful and conscious, which will inevitably be reflected in your savings.

You'll gain greater self-awareness and control, knowing what you need and can do without.

46

Giving & Generosity

Money as a tool for impact

EARNING / SPENDING

Offer What Served You

📅 **QUARTERLY**   🕐 **15 MIN**

The world is strange, sometimes behaving in ways we can't quite explain. One typical pattern involves the rule of giving: the more you give, the more you seem to receive in return, a principle also found in most religions.

This habit helps you put it into practice in your daily life while giving your money a more generous, purposeful meaning.

Every quarter, you'll identify a product that greatly benefited and impacted your skills, mindset, or income. It could be anything, from a deeply informative book to a great lecture series or online training.

Once identified, you will offer it to someone else who seems to be starting their development journey or simply who could learn from it.

Make the offering heartfelt and genuine. Add a small note explaining what the gift means to you and how best to extract value from it.

Engaging regularly in this simple yet meaningful gesture of generosity not only builds a positive, abundant mindset, but also allows those around you to benefit, enriching your social environment.

47

Giving & Generosity

Money as a tool for impact

INVESTING

Invest in Causes You Trust

📅 **MONTHLY**　🕐 **30 MIN**

You know what's more important than money? Purpose. If you have a solid vision, passion, and deep meaning, working does not feel like working, and the money often automatically follows.

This habit aligns investment with a meaningful purpose, to give you reasons to invest and hold onto your investment.

Each month, allocate 5% of your savings to a dedicated cause, focusing on creating good in this world. Whether that good is clean energy, social equity funds, or educational tech is up to you. But it must be something beyond yourself, something bigger, positively impacting the lives of others.

You can also track your investment's progress in a dashboard or journal. Ensure you include profit and impact performance metrics so you don't lose sight of the bigger picture.

Such a habit makes your money work for everyone rather than just for yourself. It expands horizons and helps you pursue a more significant goal than simple wealth building.

48

Giving & Generosity

Money as a tool for impact

MINDSET / IMPACT

Give Without Expecting Anything in Return

📅 **MONTHLY**   🕐 **30 MIN**

The greatest fulfillment of life is in giving, not taking. And until you've experienced this first-hand, you haven't really lived.

What could be called the *Invisible Giving Ritual* is a great way to practice generosity without expectations.

Once a month, engage in an anonymous gifting act. Spend your money, time, or effort for the benefit of someone else.

For example, you could pay for a stranger's coffee or quietly leave a gift on someone's doorstep. The choice is yours, as long as the act remains hidden.

Later, you can journal how it made you feel and what feeling you hope it created for the receiver. More than the outcome, the emotional richness it stirred up within you is essential. You'll be surprised how powerful a simple gesture of kindness can be.

The *Invisible Giving Ritual* makes you wealthy from the inside rather than the outside. Regularly following this practice instills a deep-rooted generosity in your identity, making it a natural part of who you are.

MENTAL

Develop mental clarity to build self-confidence,
deepen calm, and sharpen your focus.

49

Present-moment

Awareness and mindfulness practices

MINDFULNESS

Be Present in the Moment

📅 **DAILY**   🕐 **20 MIN**

Your mind is a rambling machine, and training it to sit still requires focus, dedication, and mindfulness.

The *Colors of the Walk* meditation is a fun and easy way to quiet the noise within your mind and meditate without needing to stay still.

Each day, choose three colors before beginning your twenty-minute walk. During that walk, identify as many of your chosen three colors as possible in the things surrounding you.

This simple habit helps turn each step of your walk into a conscious moment, preventing your mind from shifting into autopilot or worrying.

The *Colors of the Walk* meditation method is excellent for people who find common sitting meditation boring.

By converting mindfulness into a fun visual treasure hunt, you gain control of your brain and build real-time focus and awareness of your environment.

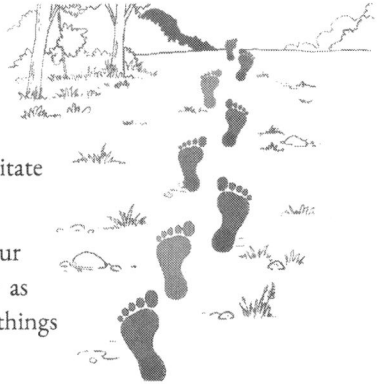

50

Present-moment
Awareness and mindfulness practices

BELIEFS

Prove Your Self-Limiting Beliefs Wrong

WEEKLY   **30 MIN**

The way you view yourself determines who you are. If you want to be successful, you must first learn to view yourself as such.

Every week, self-reflect and choose one self-limiting belief you wish to change. It could be anything, such as: *"I'm not creative enough,"* or *"I don't know how to handle money wisely."*

Once you've chosen the belief, it's time to convince your mind to eliminate it.

Throughout each day of that week, carefully consider everything you do that contradicts that limiting belief. Every action, experience, and observation that goes against it. And at the end of the day, note them all down in a journal.

For example, you could be someone who views themselves as an underconfident team player, noting how you successfully led a delegation of five to complete a project.

Writing down all your small victories in this manner will slowly change how you see yourself, making you realize there's more to you than you thought. That self-limiting belief will soon be washed away entirely, and when it is, you can begin working on another one in the next week.

This habit shifts your internal narrative to develop a growth mindset and positivity.

Present-moment
Awareness and mindfulness practices

LEARNING

Break Your Routines

📅 **DAILY**　　🕐 **5 MIN**

If you're not careful, life can turn into a never-ending loop, draining you of creativity and adventure.

Every day, you wake up at the same time, have the same breakfast, drive to work using the same route, and interact with the same people in the same way, only to come home and sleep before doing it all again the next day. It is called routine, and it is boring.

This habit helps you break the numbing cycle and introduces newness to your life. Here is how you practice it:

Each day, choose one small part of your daily routine and break it, doing something different instead. That difference could be anything, for example:

- Driving to work on a different route
- Eating an entirely new breakfast
- Listening to totally different music
- Switching up your morning routine
- Avoid using a specific word that you think sounds negative

Right after finishing your chosen task, notice how conscious you felt when you did it, how many new things you saw, and how your alertness suddenly shifted. You may write down your reflections in a journal for motivation and inspiration.

The *Routine Breaker* helps spice up life, avoid mundane repetitiveness, and invigorate your day with new energy and curiosity. It allows you to gain a whole new appreciation and outlook on your surroundings.

52

Journaling

Reflection and self-discovery

MINDFULNESS

Understand Daily Life Patterns

📅 **DAILY**   🕐 **10 MIN**

Your life's meaning really only matters if you pay attention to it. If you're truly attentive, awareness helps you catch moments that can contribute to your personal growth.

Stimulate your life with a fresh dose of meaning, uncovering emotional patterns to grow self-awareness.

Every day, write a vivid description of the most impactful moment you experienced during the day.

As an introduction to your writing, take three long, intentional breaths and immediately write down a single sentence describing the moment you are trying to catch.

Focus on the small, raw details: where you were, what you felt, the sensations in your body, and the subtle energy of space around you. Let it happen intuitively and naturally, like inspiration flowing from you to the page. Let your heart guide the pen and place your complete trust in it.

Review your snapshots and reflect on them at the end of the week, taking careful mental notes of the main emotional themes in the moments you captured and what triggered them.

This habit helps you build emotional awareness and uncover blind spots through a simple self-reflective method.

53

Journaling

Reflection and self-discovery

BELIEFS

Be Driven by Who You Want to Become

📅 **MONTHLY**   🕐 **10 MIN**

Have you ever wondered how you will be different in 10 years?

Setting long-term goals for yourself is essential to make informed mid- and short-term decisions and grow in the right direction.

Write a message from your future self every month — imagining it's you, ten years older.

- What would he/she say about the way you live today?
- What advice would he/she give?
- What would he/she want you to achieve?
- What would he/she tell you to let go of?
- What would he/she ask you to focus on?

Make sure the letter is encouraging and motivational. You should feel a surge of optimism when reading it and a new sense of anticipation for tomorrow.

Such a habit helps you set goals, reflect on how to use your present and future to the best advantage, and encourages you to think maturely.

Regularly practicing this transforms your perspective on life, adds meaningfulness, and expands your horizons, enlarging possibilities.

54

Journaling

Reflection and self-discovery

LEARNING

Collect Life Lessons and Let Them Shape You

📅 WEEKLY   🕐 5 MIN

If you've failed a hundred times and learned something from each failure, you'll be far better off than someone who succeeded once but never bothered to learn anything from it.

This habit helps you record uncovered truths, forcing you to remember them and shape your perspective on the world.

At the end of every week, write down meaningful insights you gained relating to yourself, someone else, or the world in general during that week. It doesn't have to be groundbreaking. Even a moment of quiet reflection or a small, secret victory is enough if it teaches you something. Ideally, the thought should be summarized in a simple sentence.

Store your learnings in a journal to reflect upon at the end of every month, highlighting the main lesson of the month. This will ensure that valuable lessons are cemented in your personality, shaping your mind with structure.

55

Stress Management

Coping mechanisms and calming techniques

MINDFULNESS

Prepare for Stressful Situations

🗓️ **DAILY**   🕐 **5 MIN**

Stress is not just a state of mind; it's a full-body event. And just like a fire extinguisher is useless if you don't know where it is or how to use it, stress relief tools only work if they're practiced and ready.

This habit involves preparing stress-relief items to help you intentionally de-escalate stress.

First, assemble your personal toolkit. Include 3–5 items that help regulate your nervous system through direct sensory inputs.

Examples could include:

- A cold compress or cooling roller for your neck (vagus nerve deactivation)
- A small bottle of calming essential oil (such as lavender or peppermint)
- A textured stress ball or hand grip
- Earbuds preloaded with a calming playlist
- A metronome or breathing app for paced breathing

Prepare this stress defense system in a drawer of your desk, a box, or a bag, so that you can easily reach for it when your stress starts rising.

Practice using your toolkit during light stress moments—not just during breakdowns—so your body can recognize these tools as a safe and effective way to respond.

This habit gives you control and relieves stress before it hijacks your mind or body.

56

Stress Management

Coping mechanisms and calming techniques

BELIEFS

Free Yourself from Self-Bias Systems

📅 **WEEKLY**   🕐 **10 MIN**

Being kind and compassionate towards others is undoubtedly essential. But what about toward yourself? Are you a friend to yourself, or do you act with tyranny?

This habit is a simple way to free you from self-imposed bias.

Each week, identify one "contract" you made with yourself that is now rooted so profoundly that it is tied to you. It could be anything, such as:

- I always need to be available for my friends
- All my work needs to be flawless and on time
- I'm not a good leader
- Rest is earned, not given

In place of one of these unfair contracts, write down a different, more understanding one. Something easier and more practical to follow. For example:

- I'll try to be available for my friends if it doesn't take over my feelings of privacy
- My work should be done with my best effort, but mistakes are human nature
- I will focus on communication and decision-making to inspire my team
- Rest is a requirement, not a privilege to be earned.

The new principle will be hung on your personal whiteboard, in your office, or at home to remind you of your area of focus for the coming weeks. Over time, it will help you eliminate incorrect self-beliefs and adopt new ones that are more effective and compassionate towards yourself.

57

Stress Management

Coping mechanisms and calming techniques

LEARNING

Identify Stress Symptoms and Ease Them

DAILY   **5 MIN**

If your mind is the invisible author of your thoughts, your body is the canvas upon which it conducts its work. One great way to know what state your mind is in is to ask your body.

This method is a body mapping diagnosis exercise, with which you will:

1. Draw a figure representing yourself on a piece of paper.
2. Take 5 minutes to audit your body's feelings, focusing on one part at a time.
3. Label each body part on the paper according to how you feel (e.g., tension, pain, etc.)

Once your self-diagnosis is completed, it's time to act. Based on the issues identified in your self-diagnosis, develop routines to address and eliminate them.

Common Issues	Solution
Neck Stiffness	Gentle neck rolls and heat pack application.
Tight Shoulders	Shoulder shrugs and deep chest breathing.
Lower Back Pain	Cat-cow stretches and lumbar support improvements.
Tense Forehead	Forehead massage and intentional blinking breaks.
Heavy Chest	Diaphragmatic (belly) breathing exercises.
Hand Tension	Finger stretches and periodic self-handshakes.
Tight Hips	Seated hip openers and standing walk breaks.
Leg Restlessness	Ankle circles and mini-walking sessions.
Foot Soreness	Tennis ball foot massage and calf stretches.
Stomach Discomfort	Slow, deep breathing and mindful eating habits.

This diagnosis method is excellent for developing health awareness and remedying discomfort. Do this each week to ensure your body remains pleasantly light.

58

Growth Mindset

Embracing change and learning

MINDFULNESS

Apply the 3 Ps

DAILY   **5 MIN**

Developing a growth mindset is critical to success in any goal in life.

Use the 3 Ps method to become the best version of yourself and transform negative thinking into learning opportunities.

Each time a negative or limiting thought arises, take the following steps:

1. **P**ause—Acknowledge the thought's existence and then write it down to reduce its power.
2. **P**ivot—Ask yourself: Does this thought belong to your future? What and how can you learn from this thought?
3. **P**erspective—In a single, concise sentence, turn the thought from an obstacle into an opportunity for learning and growth.

Regularly engaging in the 3Ps habit and revisiting your notes weekly is a great way to develop a better mindset, never letting go of positivity, and growing towards the best version of yourself.

59
Growth Mindset
Embracing change and learning

BELIEFS

Grow Empowering Beliefs

📅 **MONTHLY**   🕐 **30 MIN**

The kind of person you'll grow up to be is decided not just by you but by those around you. Your family, friends, and peers play a pivotal role in planting the seeds that will eventually flower into your future personality.

BEHAVIORS

BELIEFS

Not all seeds are healthy, however. Some can sprout negative roots. And the *Belief Mapping Tree* shifts negative perceptions about yourself into positive perceptions.

Draw a diagram of a tree. Once done, begin labelling its roots. Each root label should highlight a particular experience in your early childhood that planted a limiting belief. Being scolded by your parents, facing bullies at school, or struggling with your body are a few examples of such experiences.

Once you've labelled the roots, turn to the branches. Each branch represents a behavioral consequence of the experience that developed limiting beliefs. For example, a pessimistic outlook, a lack of confidence, or social anxiety are all examples of limiting beliefs.

Once this is done, make another tree identical to the first, with the root labelled with a growth opportunity, empowering you to remove the limiting belief you placed on the first tree.

Now, label branches of your second tree with positive outcomes from the new growth opportunity.

The Belief Mapping exercise is a great visual technique to shift your perspective and reset self-limiting beliefs. Pessimism is replaced by optimistic thinking.

60

Growth Mindset

Embracing change and learning

LEARNING

Learn From Your Proximity Circle

📅 **WEEKLY**   🕐 **1 HOUR**

Many people overlook the power of collaborating with like-minded individuals to develop and learn. The more you know, the more you grow in life and become available to new possibilities.

Choose a friend, partner, or colleague each week and schedule a one-hour skill-exchange meeting.

During this meeting, each participant teaches the other an easy skill. It could be anything, from playing an instrument to setting up an *Excel* spreadsheet or going over your favorite websites and apps.

To keep things fresh and alive, change the "buddy" frequently so that you're always learning new kinds of skills from different people.

Apart from learning something new, it's a fun way to engage in social activities and maintain a spirit of curiosity, which could lead to a lifelong passion - who knows?

By learning from a diverse set of people, you equip yourself with a broad skill set that may prove to be useful and complement the ones you already have.

61

Decluttering the Mind

Reducing noise and negative inputs

MINDFULNESS

Reduce the Pace to Think Clearly

📅 **WEEKLY**   🕐 **2 HOURS**

Slowing down has been proven to be beneficial for your own mind, and it is essential to practice slowness to avoid mental breakdown.

This Social Meditation method can be practiced anywhere and at any time. It's a great way to slow down and give your mind and body time to process things, allowing you to adjust to a more relaxed pace.

During a 2-hour window, at least every week, soften every aspect of yourself:

- Turn your voice one tone down.
- Make your regular movements slower, such as walking and interacting with objects.
- Breathe lightly and consciously.
- Pause for three seconds before responding to someone.
- Remove sharp noises and harsh lights from the environment.

This Social Meditation method allows to immerse yourself in an environment that naturally encourages a slower pace and a meditative state.

Lowering your overall intensity and softening sensory inputs allows your mind to reduce speed organically.

It allows for more focus and reflectiveness in people's interactions, resulting in an overall reduction of stress and a more attractive aura in social interactions.

62
Decluttering the Mind
Reducing noise and negative inputs

BELIEFS

Remove Self-Limiting Beliefs and Transform Yourself

MONTHLY   **10 MIN**

Having a positive mindset starts from within, and the good news is that you can control your mind.

To become a better self, you must declutter your mind, discard all self-limiting beliefs, and grow new ones. Better ones.

Such things are easier said than done; some self-limiting beliefs are anchored so profoundly that they seem to refuse to leave your side, no matter how hard you try.

This habit is an effective way to rid yourself of persistent negative attitudes by using physical acts to train your mind to recognize and process them in the way they should be.

Over a month, write self-limiting principles on paper, with one self-limiting principle per piece of paper, and put them in a box.

After a month, reread the self-limiting beliefs and:

1. Select two to be gone forever. Such limiting beliefs (paper) will be burnt (safely) by yourself. Watch that limiting belief burn to ashes.
2. Select two to be transformed. Strike the limiting belief and rewrite a new one on the back of the paper, which you will hang on your personal board.

Watching your limiting beliefs burn makes your mind think the belief is leaving it.

Similarly, striking and rewriting a belief is an initial anchor for the mind to believe in transformation.

63

Decluttering the Mind
Reducing noise and negative inputs

LEARNING

Keep the Learning Circle Alive

WEEKLY   **10 MIN**

Growth requires learning. Learning requires consistency.

The *Learning Card Program* promotes consistent learning in a fun and engaging way, providing a framework that declutters your learning process.

How does it work?

1. Find a deck of blank cards; on each card, write down one learning you want to engage with (e.g., gardening, affiliate marketing, etc.)
2. Sort out the deck into three piles based on learning priority. On the blank side of each card, write one of the following labels:
   a. Keep Learning Now
   b. Let's Go
   c. Park for Later or Be Gone

Time to begin the game! Every Monday, draw one card from each deck.

> The Keep Learning card is placed on your desk for one month, and the activity written on it must be practiced at least once weekly.

> The Park for Later card is read and goes straight to the bottom of the Let's Go deck.

> The Let's Go card is acted upon only once that week, then either discarded or placed at the bottom of the Keep Learning Deck.

The *Learning Cards Program* is an ingenious way to organize and focus on various learning goals, ensuring progress. It also helps to think about learning topics before learning from them, turning the learning process into an exciting game of curiosity.

64

Self-Talk & Inner Dialogue

Reframing beliefs

MINDFULNESS

Develop Situational Analytic Skills

📅 DAILY   🕐 10 MIN

Every challenge in life is an opportunity to grow if you can develop efficient perceptions and analytical capabilities.

Whenever a challenging situation arises, process it through the four-columned grid containing the following labels:

1. What exactly is going on, factually and emotionally?
2. If people are involved, how might others perceive or experience this?
3. What do I know, and what might I be assuming?
4. What is the most constructive way I can respond right now to allow for more time for reflection?

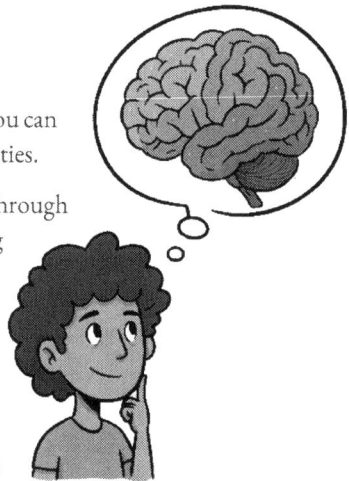

Analyze the situation and the associated thoughts and emotions, marking your findings in each of these four columns.

This method provides a standard framework to process situations efficiently, helps you avoid overthinking, and fosters a pragmatic approach to situational analysis.

Over time, it will also train your mind and emotions to handle adverse situations with more composure and objectivity rather than with impulsive reactions.

65

Self-Talk & Inner Dialogue

Reframing beliefs

BELIEFS

Challenge Your Self-Limiting Beliefs

📅 **WEEKLY**　　🕐 **15 MIN**

How many of your held beliefs are actually true? How biased do you view yourself?

If you've never considered investigating these questions, now's the time. The more you learn about yourself, the better equipped you'll be to capitalize on your strengths while working on your weaknesses. Developing an *Evidence Board* will help you on this journey.

Go deep within yourself and pick one limiting belief. Write it down on paper and pin it onto a corkboard or a notebook page. Then, for the remainder of the week, look for any experience or action that contradicts or supports that belief. Note that experience on paper and pin it on your *Evidence Board*. Use different colors to distinguish between supporting and contradicting evidence.

At the end of the week, take a closer look at your board. Which side is winning? Is your belief justified or not? Based on the evidence, either discard the unproven belief or identify the most recurring patterns of proven shortcomings and address them.

Keep the *Evidence Board* on your wall, do the same exercise in 3 months, and assess the new results the same way.

Using such a method helps you gain an understanding of yourself, rather than just mindlessly stumbling through situations holding unverified beliefs.

Knowing who you are and who you are not can help you develop self-awareness and make plans to improve yourself.

66

Self-Talk & Inner Dialogue

Reframing beliefs

LEARNING

Acknowledge Challenges to Better Overcome Them

📅 **MONTHLY**　　🕐 **10 MIN**

Adversity is like a mirror: the more positively you embrace it, the lighter adversity will feel. And the opposite is also true: the more negatively you react, the worse the problem will become.

Use a *Mind Stretch Log* to turn difficulties into opportunities. After you feel stuck-- whether while learning something, completing a task, or achieving a goal--write down these three things in your *Mind Stretch Log*.

1.　What felt hard?
2.　What belief about your learning ability did it challenge?
3.　What did you eventually understand and improve?

The *Mind Stretch Log* is your personal record of prevailing against difficulty. Each entry is a testament to your perseverance and proof of the hidden opportunities for growth lurking in every problem.

The more entries you make, the greater your confidence in your own self and the better your ability to handle tough times with optimism.

Mental Boundaries

Detaching from drama or negativity

MINDFULNESS

Know How to Protect Your Emotions

📅 **WEEKLY**   🕐 **10 MIN**

Just like you need an umbrella to protect yourself from the rain, your emotions need a similar shield against life's unexpected happenings.

The *Emotional Umbrella* method helps you establish that visual protection and cultivate awareness.

Every Monday, pick one emotion you want to preserve throughout the week, regardless of what happens around you.

Draw an umbrella and write that quality down beneath it. Then, on the umbrella's divided canopies, write down three ways through which you will ensure this protection.

Below is an example:

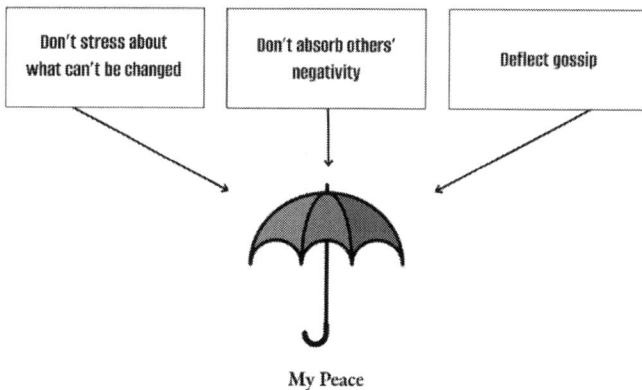

Don't stress about what can't be changed	Don't absorb others' negativity	Deflect gossip

My Peace

Living with an *Emotional Umbrella* ensures setting up principles dedicated to protecting precious emotions, which in turn will reinforce self-confidence and assertiveness.

68

Mental Boundaries

Detaching from drama or negativity

BELIEFS

Build Emotional Boundaries

WEEKLY   **10 MIN**

The more you practice something, the more it becomes a habit. The *One Principle Card* method helps you implement principles and consistently live by your values.

Every week, pick a principle that you want to embody. It could be anything, from *"I'm not allowing anyone to distract me"* to *"I'm not afraid to say no."*

Write this principle down on a small card, and then, beneath it, write three responses you will give if you feel it triggered.

The card could also include affirmation reminders, mindset shifts, or even short breaks to recalibrate your state of mind.

Carry your *One Principle Card* with you during the entire week. Feeling its weight in your pocket will serve as a physical reminder, helping you stay aware of the chosen principle and reframing any sub-principles. You may also refer to it at any time.

Keeping the principle on a card close to you will force the principle to penetrate deeply into your subconscious and stick until you embody that principle naturally.

Mental Boundaries

Detaching from drama or negativity

LEARNING

Target Your Learnings

📅 **DAILY**   🕐 **15 MIN**

People often focus on hard work and intensity, but rarely reflect on the strategic aspect of the energy deployed.

Working hard is only half the way to a specific goal because working in the wrong direction does not lead to a better place. Burnt out with no results to show is not fun.

Targeted Learning improves the output of educational sessions to be more effective and productive.

Before beginning a learning session, answer the following questions:

1. What specific questions do you want to answer?
2. What related skills do you wish to develop?
3. How does your chosen topic connect with other topics you are interested in?

If you choose the training materials, you can now target your selection.

If someone imposes the training material, review the three answers at the end of the training session and ensure they have been covered completely. Now, write what you will be learning next to continue the initiated development.

Being targeted ensures that you control the direction of things you decide to implement in your life and that you are not just grinding away for the sake of it. Being focused results in an improved version of yourself.

70
Curiosity
Feeding the mind with questions and wonder

MINDFULNESS

Handle Conflictual Interaction with Wisdom

🗓 **DAILY**   🕐 **5 MIN**

Conflictual human interaction is probably the most challenging aspect of life to deal with. One moment is all it takes to make a difference when responding to a difficult interaction.

This habit provides a framework for calmly and consciously analyzing and addressing challenging human interactions.

Given that interacting with others involves, by definition, live interactions, you will need to learn the three questions by heart and practice answering them quickly in your mind during challenging interactions for the method to be fully efficient.

You may, however, start by writing them on a piece of paper which you can keep with you for easy reference, to force your memory:

1. What are the people involved likely thinking?
2. Could the opposite of my current thinking also be true?
3. How can I turn my reaction into one that will be perceived positively, with enough space for more discussion?

Allowing yourself a brief pause before answering, particularly in a heated exchange, will always be perceived as reflective, often resulting in greater consideration by the "opposite" side.

Regular practice of this habit helps you transform impulsion into conscious responses.

Curiosity

Feeding the mind with questions and wonder

BELIEFS

Map Out Your Beliefs

📅 **MONTHLY**   🕐 **15 MIN**

The beauty in life is that the personal growth journey never ends. Every part of us constantly evolves, including our values and beliefs.

The *Belief Playground Map* is a fun, creative way to map your beliefs and values and make changes over time.

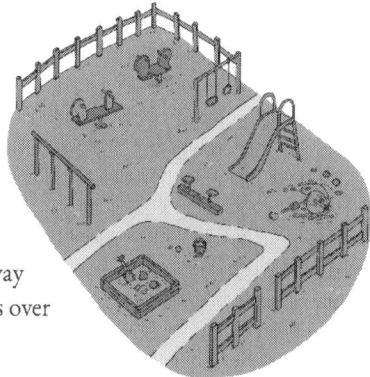

Simply take an A3 blank white page and draw a playground with five different zones. Next to each zone, there will be specific elements paired as per the instructions below:

1. **See-Saws**: These represent your conflicting beliefs. Those you are not sure about yet.
2. **Slides**: These are beliefs you've outgrown. Those you no longer believe in.
3. **Sandboxes**: These are beliefs you're still testing, usually newer ones you are still not 100% sure about.
4. **Monkey Bars**: These are more complex beliefs you trust but which you're still struggling to grasp fully.
5. **Fences**: These are boundaries you've chosen to maintain. List the most important ones. You can have only 4.

Each month, visit this personal playground of yours and explore it. See if anything needs to move from one place to another, be added, or completely removed.

Have you acquired any new beliefs or existing ones? Have any of your beliefs strengthened or been challenged? Update the playground as needed, gaining a fresh perspective of yourself.

The *Belief Playground Map* is an easy and very visual way to reinforce your inner self and acknowledge how you change over time.

72

Curiosity
Feeding the mind with questions and wonder

LEARNING

Track Your Curiosity and Feed It

WEEKLY   **30 MIN**

Have you ever paid attention to the way children behave? How unflinchingly curious are they about everything around them, constantly peppering their parents with questions? That spark of curiosity slowly fades out, entirely disappearing by the time adulthood comes along.

Maintaining a *Curiosity Tracker* is a simple habit that helps you revive that spark again.

Every time a question bubbles up to the surface of your mind, write it down rather than ignoring it. It doesn't matter how trivial or irrelevant the question might be; note it in your journal or an app.

At the end of the week, revisit your notes, pick one curiosity seed, spend 30 minutes learning about it, and log your findings in a separate journal.

The *Curiosity Seeds Tracker* is a great way to cultivate curiosity and learn to appreciate things, which can significantly enhance your personal development journey.

PHYSICAL

Strengthen your body to live with energy,
daily resilience, and in tune with yourself.

Light Activity

Walking, stretching, daily movement

MOVEMENT

Avoid Office Syndrome

DAILY   **15 MIN**

Today, the modern workplace often means your home, which was not always designed with comfort in mind for working.

As a result, more and more people suffer from "Office Syndrome", which is physical discomfort caused by prolonged sitting hours, poor posture, and extensive screen time with little movement.

This habit helps avoid all that. Create a "Movement Plan", which includes 3 to 5 ways to reset your body out of this list:

- Take a fake commute walk in the morning, at lunchtime, and at the end of the afternoon to stretch your legs, as you would if you were going to work or lunch.
- Keep a tennis ball or foot roller under your desk for unconscious foot massages.
- Set a timer every hour to engage in a quick 5-minute stretch of your neck, back, and hips.
- Reset your eyes every half-hour by leaving your screen and looking out a window at a distant object. No need to leave your chair.
- Use the phone-call pacing rule, which requires standing up and walking around each time you're on a call.
- Use Post-it prompts, placed on your desk or in a notebook you often consult, to remind you of things like "Stretch Your Spine" or "Loosen Your Hips".

Remaining physically active and fluid during office hours benefits not just your health but your productivity as well.

74
Light Activity
Walking, stretching, daily movement

NUTRITION

Drink-Then-Do, Stretch-Then-Snack

📅 **DAILY**   🕐 **10 MIN**

Habits do not need to be complicated to be efficient. It is more often in the simplicity of things done with consistency.

Your body functions differently at various times of the day, and simple habits can be even more effective if timed appropriately.

The *Drink-Then-Do, Stretch-Then-Snack* encapsulates this concept with two efficient ideas:

1. **Drink-Then-Do**: When you wake up in the morning, before doing anything, drink a large glass of water with turmeric, Himalayan salt, half a lemon, a spoonful of olive oil, paprika, apple cider, and ginger. Essentially a mix of antioxidants, minerals, and healthy fats, it boosts digestion, reduces inflammation, supports hydration, and enhances metabolism to support your day.

2. **Stretch-Then-Snack**: Each time you crave a snack, engage in a minute of light activity first. The activity could be anything, ranging from full-body stretches to a short cardio session. Keep it fresh by switching up routines. It helps create positive associations, strengthen self-discipline, and reduce mindless snacking.

Remember, whatever habit you implement, ensure it has a positive effect and maintains consistency. The compounding effect will consistently outperform short-lived intensity.

75

Light Activity

Walking, stretching, daily movement

HEALTH

Listen to Your Body

📅 **WEEKLY**   🕐 **30 MIN**

You might find this hard to believe, but your body constantly speaks to you, telling you how it feels and what it needs. But those words often get disregarded and lost in the business of life.

This habit is your weekly sit-in with your body. Remove all else from your calendar and take your mind off your worries.

Sit down with your body and begin to ask how it feels. Take inventory of your muscles, joints, and bones, and check how they are. Is there any soreness, fatigue, or pain? Or any other strange sensations? Does your body feel relaxed and energized or strangely tense and off-kilter?

Create a *Body Log* using various categories, such as posture, flexibility, digestion, pain, and fatigue, and note each part of your physical anatomy and its condition. Color codes them for more straightforward interpretation.

⚪ = *Feels Good*

🔘 = *Mild Discomfort or pain*

⚫ = *Moderate to severe pain and discomfort*

Monitoring your physical state every week is a great way to become more aware of your well-being, take preventive measures, and care for yourself.

Many people have no problem overloading their time with meetings and professional obligations, but struggle to take 30 minutes to check in with themselves.

Physical Routine

Strength, endurance, or flexibility

MOVEMENT

Repeat Consistently to Beat Intensity

📅 **DAILY**   🕐 **5 MIN**

The power is in repetition, regardless of how small what you repeat is. The mind and body function in pairs, influencing each other in ways that could form a virtuous or vicious circle. Taking care of both is essential.

Use the *5*5*5 Strengthening Method* to keep your body well without sacrificing much from your day. Perform five simple bodyweight exercises (e.g., push-ups, planks, squats) for just 5 minutes a day, 5 days a week. The reps must be tailored to your fitness levels to ensure the exercises are at a minimum challenging level.

The *5*5*5 challenge* requires very little commitment and virtually no extra equipment.

If practiced regularly, the benefits will be evident in both your body and mind. Taking a small window of time each day to engage in physical activity will boost dopamine levels, reduce the risk of chronic diseases, and give your mind the break it deserves while continuing to strengthen your muscles.

Physical Routine

Strength, endurance, or flexibility

NUTRITION

Be Intentional in Choosing What You Eat

📅 **DAILY**   🕐 **10 MIN**

You are what you eat, and who you are determines how your life will be. So, better eat well.

This habit is an intuitive and hassle-free way to add healthy eating into your routine and empower yourself for successful living. All you need to do is the following:

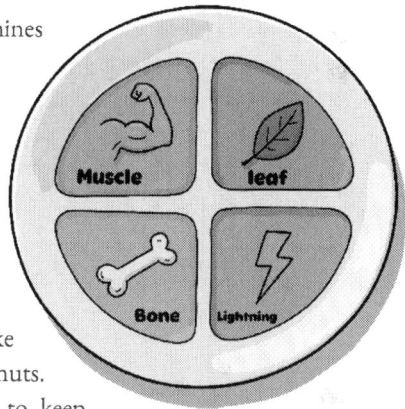

1. Create an *Energy Shelf* in your fridge exclusively dedicated to high-protein and nutrient-dense foods like eggs, lentils, tuna, yogurt, tofu, or nuts. Rotate the food items every week to keep things interesting and fresh.

2. Next, use this nutritive rule for each meal of your day: Build your plate around one item chosen from your energy shelf, letting that food item take the lead. Then, compose around it.

This habit is about getting organized around future intake. It makes healthy eating natural and eliminates unhealthy shortcuts. All you have to do is pick one nutrient-dense item and build around it.

78

Physical Routine

Strength, endurance, or flexibility

HEALTH

Develop Mind Clarity and Memory by Sleeping Well

📅 DAILY   🕐 5 MIN

Resting is an art, not a power-off button for your body. If you want to perform optimally, how well you sleep is just as crucial as how much.

This habit revolves around sleeping quality:

1. **Night-Prep**: Begin winding down 30 minutes before bed, ensuring you don't engage in any focused physical or mental activity afterward. Cut out screens 45 minutes before bed, and make sure your last meal is at least 2 hours before you plan to sleep. Sip on a light herbal or ginger tea to help relax your body and mind.
   Benefits: This habit enhances sleep quality, facilitating a smoother mind-body transition into rest, and supports digestion by reducing stimulation.
2. **Morning-Prep**: The morning after sleep is almost as important as the sleep itself. Start your day without a phone for at least the first hour. When you wake up, write a free page in your journal summarizing what you dreamt of. After your shower, go outside and expose yourself to natural light for 5 minutes, barefoot if possible, looking at the sky (away from the sun) to calibrate your eyes to the horizon.
   Benefits: This morning prep helps enhance mental clarity and memory, regulates your body clock, and improves sleep quality by reducing overstimulation.
3. Track sleep quality through an app.

Effective resting prevents burnout, speeds up recovery, and helps you gain vitality.

Sleep Hygiene

Deep, restorative sleep

MOVEMENT

Use Gravity to Exercise Lightly

DAILY   **15 MIN**

If your dreams are troubled and your sleep feels more tiring than restful, it might be time to reconsider your nighttime routine.

This ritual is one way to defuse the day's tension from your body and prepare yourself for a restful, energizing sleep.

Here are the steps:

1. **Mindful Movements**: Take a 5-minute walk outdoors (barefoot if possible, to stimulate your nerves positively) while holding a light object in your hand, weighing no more than 1 to 2 kg. Walk as slowly as possible and focus on breathing.
2. **Calming Gestures**: Next, move to a mat-only corner and sit cross-legged on a small rug or yoga mat. Very slowly and consciously, perform 2-3 calming poses, such as the lotus posture, lying twists, or a knees-to-chest position. Go to sleep once it is done.

This grounding ritual utilizes gravity as a gentle strength to help your body unwind on both a muscular and psychosomatic level.

These mindful exercises help regulate the nervous system, reduce excessive cortisol production, and promote better sleep.

80

Sleep Hygiene

Deep, restorative sleep

NUTRITION

Prepare Your Mind for a Restful Night

🗓️ **DAILY**   🕐 **5 MIN**

The first 80% of your day should be spent building the future and enjoying the present. The last 20% should be spent preparing for a restful recovery to help you be effective in the 80% the next day.

You can signal sleeping as a mindful evening routine, readying you for a night of rejuvenating sleep.

1. **Last intake**: At least 2 hours before bed, ensure you combine complex carbs and tryptophan-dense foods (such as a banana with almond butter, oats with yogurt, or brown rice with turkey). Top it off with soothing herbal tea and honey, water with magnesium drops, or warm almond milk.

2. **Signals**: Switch off all kitchen lights and digital displays, signaling the end of food and screen consumption. Decreased sensory input stimulates melatonin production and naturally induces a state of early drowsiness.

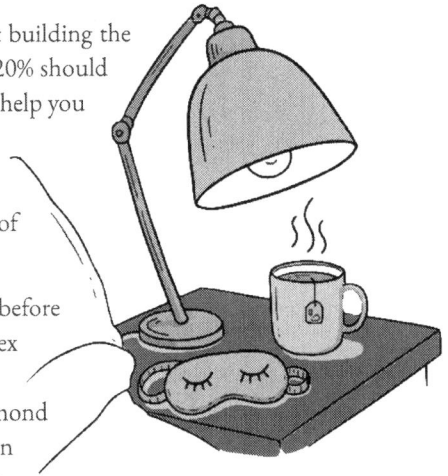

Such a habit sends unconscious signs to the mind that sleeping is near and intake has ended, mentally preparing yourself for bedtime. It is an easy way to begin winding down as the evening starts.

81

Sleep Hygiene
Deep, restorative sleep

HEALTH

Breathe Properly to Enhance Sleeping

📅 **DAILY**   🕐 **10 MIN**

Breathing well is the foundation of a good night's sleep. Yet, not many habits stimulate this aspect of sleep quality.

This sleep-enhancing ritual aims to optimize your sleeping time through better breathing.

1. First, clear your nasal passages with a warm steam bowl and a drop of essential oil, such as eucalyptus. Take slow, deep breaths for 3 minutes, clearing your nasal passages and signaling to your body and mind that sleep is near.
2. Next, avoid any inflammatory foods before sleeping, no matter how much your body craves them. Substituting this type of food with a drink is a good way to soothe your stomach and reduce hunger: try turmeric tea, ginger water, or chamomile with lemon. Something light and cleansing.
3. Finally, when lying down to sleep, ensure your posture is optimized for breathing. Lie on your left side, with a pillow between your knees and under your head, keeping your spine in a neutral position. Avoid lying flat on top of your stomach.

Centered on breathing quality, the Sleep-Enhancing Ritual enables your body and mind to derive the most benefit from a night's sleep.

Breathing & Posture
Oxygen and alignment

MOVEMENT

Maintain Healthy Postures

📅 **DAILY**   🕐 **15 MIN**

Oxygen is a vital life force for our body, just like food and water, but unfortunately, it's often overlooked.

This habit is a great way to practice easy and beneficial mindful breathing techniques.

Every day, practice:

1. **Wall Posture Reset**: Stand with your back against a wall for 2 minutes, aligning your head, shoulders, and hips into a single straight line before beginning to breathe deeply.
2. **Chest-Breath Mobility Flow**: Next, continue breathing in the same position, but this time incorporate movements such as cactus arms, side bends, and backbends for approximately 2 minutes each.
3. **Balancing Breath Challenge**: Finish the exercise by standing on one leg and taking 5-10 slow, nasal breaths with your hands on your rib cage. Do this with each leg.

This Breath and Posture ritual expands your body's oxygen intake, stimulating your lymphatic system and strengthening your immune response.

Regular practice also reduces muscle tension and pain, allowing for better posture throughout the day and maintaining a calm body.

83

Breathing & Posture
Oxygen and alignment

NUTRITION

Eat with Your Breathing in Mind

📅 **DAILY** 🕐 **10 MIN**

Exercising for health whilst eating unhealthily is like trying to empty a drowning boat with a hole in its center: for each bucketful of water you throw out, two more buckets will be waiting for you by the time you're done. The problems will never end, only multiply.

Food has specific benefits, so it is crucial to target benefits based on the aspect of our body we want to improve or stimulate. Antioxidant-rich foods are known to improve lung health, supporting better respiratory function.

Each day, craft your diet to include a salad composed of lung-supportive ingredients such as:

- **Leafy greens** (e.g., spinach, arugula, kale – rich in magnesium and nitrates to support oxygen flow)
- **Roasted beets** (enhance blood oxygenation)
- **Citrus** (high in vitamin C to reduce inflammation)
- **Seaweed** (mineral-rich and supports respiratory function)
- **Pumpkin or sunflower seeds** (provide zinc and magnesium for lung health)
- **Avocado** (healthy fats with anti-inflammatory effects)

Dress with:

- Extra virgin olive oil
- Apple cider vinegar
- Fresh lemon juice
- A pinch of black pepper
- A dash of raw honey (optional, for throat-soothing properties)

Quite obviously, eating such a composition only once will not mean a magic effect. However, a consistent intake of food benefiting a specific aspect of your body will improve it over time.

84

Breathing & Posture
Oxygen and alignment

HEALTH

Keep Your Spine Healthy

📅 **DAILY**   🕐 **10 MIN**

Decompressing the spine and improving your posture are key aspects of breathing well.

Practice daily; the *Daily Breath & Spine Reset* helps stretch the spine efficiently:

1. **Wall Melting Stretch**: Once during the day, stand up with your back flat against the wall, press your lower back against it, and slowly go down into a squat position to hold for 15 seconds, breathing heavily, before going back up.
2. **Spinal Decompression Wind-Down**: In the evenings, once home from the office, lie on your back with your legs elevated on a chair for 5-10 minutes, breathing deeply through your diaphragm into your belly.
3. **Lazy Cat on a Couch**: Sit on a couch with your feet flat, hands resting on your knees, and your back relaxed with a slight arch. As you inhale deeply, lift your chest, raise your arms, and look as high as possible up. Bringing your arms down, exhale deeply, rounding your back fully, chin to chest, and pulling your belly in.

These simple exercises stimulate spinal mobility and flexibility, preventing body stiffness.

85

Nature
Recharging through natural elements

MOVEMENT

Connect With Nature Through Meditation

📅 **DAILY**   🕐 **2 MIN**

Reconnecting with simplicity is rewarding. Nature-based meditation calms the mind and allows you to connect with your senses in meaningful ways. Even simple practices like walking barefoot on warm sands have sensorial benefits that make human beings feel completely reconnected to nature.

Concentrating on natural elements has a meditative effect, and this habit offers a meditation technique, reconnecting you with nature.

At sunrise, sit on a comfortable mat, facing east, with your legs crossed and your spine straight. Close your eyes and follow this flow quietly:

1. **Wind Awareness**: Feel the wind on your skin and guess where it comes from: north, south, east, or west.
2. **Soundscape Connection**: Now connect with the soundscape surrounding you, starting with the sound farthest away from you. Take a minute to connect with it, as it will require attention. Label it after identifying it. Next, gradually connect and label sounds that are closer to you, starting from the farthest away and working your way to the nearest.
3. **Scent Identification**: Inhale and exhale slowly. Smell and label what you recognize.
4. **Touch & Texture**: Slowly place your hand on the ground, naming the objects in your hand that you touch.

This meditative practice allows you to become more receptive to your surroundings and reconnect with yourself while maintaining a healthy posture.

86

Nature

Recharging through natural elements

NUTRITION

Connect With Nature as Often as Possible

📅 **DAILY**   🕐 **30 MIN**

When in doubt, return to the basics. This little piece of advice applies to all aspects of life, including your physical and mental well-being. When you feel your energy draining and focus slipping, it's time to reconnect with simplicity.

This experience is simple and brings nature back to your plate. Literally.

Every day, pick three seasonal food items (rotating the selection as much as possible), such as fruit or nuts. Place them in a naturally made container (e.g., wooden plate) and consume them in natural light, preferably outdoors. You could use your balcony, garden, or sit outside in natural, public spaces.

With your meal, it's essential to slow down and become aware of every sensation. The fruit's moist, citrusy flavor on your tongue, its smell, and its texture. Feel it all.

With it, enjoy a hot drink or fresh seasonal fruit juice, depending on the weather, and ensure the cup remains made of natural material (rather than plastic) to keep the experience as connected to nature as possible and authentic.

This habit may sound simple, but when was the last time you did something like it? Our mind is made to be attracted by complexity, while pleasure is found in simplicity.

More than just the seasonal fruit benefits and growing awareness of seasonality, maintaining mindfulness of the present moment allows your mind to declutter, empowering it with greater focus and calm.

87

Nature

Recharging through natural elements

HEALTH

Meditate to Self-Diagnosis How Your Body Feels

📅 **WEEKLY**   🕐 **15 MIN**

Your body was always meant to remain in sync with nature, and whenever you feel a little down, the outdoors is the best place to go for some good advice.

Each week, or at least once every two weeks, engage in a mindful bodily awareness session in a natural, outdoor setting. Ensure you're somewhere with plenty of greenery, an open passage for the wind, and abundant natural light.

Lying down on a mat, conduct a self-body scan meditation for 10-15 minutes, moving your attention slowly, starting from your head and working your way down along your body, to the tips of your toes. While doing this, analyze how you feel about each part with precise adjectives.

Whenever your mind wanders, gently pull it back and continue your scan to cover your entire body. Keep a mild focus on the physical sounds and sensations around you to maintain your mindful attention.

After the session, write down your findings as a doctor would and develop a plan to remediate the potential issues you uncovered.

This self-diagnosis exercise is an intuitive way to reconnect with yourself and become more aware of your body's needs.

88

Limiting Substances

Alcohol, sugar, stimulants

MOVEMENT

Combine Consistency and Intensity

📅 **DAILY**   🕐 **30 MIN**

It's better to do something with 50% effort every day than with 100% effort once a week.

Remember this adage about habits: consistency always beats intensity.

Health is no exception.

This habit effectively suggests combining consistency and intensity to maximize the positive effect of body sweat in a limited time. The routine was designed for busy people:

1. Every morning, begin with 15 to 20 minutes of 3 to 4 high-intensity cardio exercises of 5 minutes each (e.g., jumping rope, sprint running, fast swimming, or stairs running)
2. Next, hold a squat against a wall for 4 minutes to activate your core and stimulate your organs.
3. Finally, end with a Hot-Cool Cycle Shower: alternate between 30 seconds of hot water and 30 seconds of cold water for 3 minutes.

It helps flush toxins from your body, boosts metabolic functions, and releases endorphins, which can positively affect your mood.

Limiting Substances

Alcohol, sugar, stimulants

NUTRITION

Anticipate Your Craving Weaknesses

📅 **DAILY** 🕐 **5 MIN**

If you're struggling to avoid unhealthy food and sugar, setting healthy habits around them is a great start and a better approach than relying solely on your willpower. Let's devise an innovative and strategic game plan.

The *PRS Craving* method is a straightforward and effective way to overcome unhealthy impulses. You can break it down into a three-part ritual:

1. **Prevention**: If snacking on unhealthy foods can't be avoided, being prepared with healthier alternatives is always better. Keep stabilizing snacks, like hummus, almonds, or healthy bars, within easy reach and in reasonable portions.

2. **Replacement**: Whenever cravings are more substantial, prepare a sensory-rich alternative, such as banana cacao mousse or a mint-lime herbal spritzer, to help curb hunger. It will help you maintain a healthy diet.

3. **Stimulation**: Another trick is to use a punishment, albeit a mild one, if you must give in to unhealthy snacking. Use a bitter food, such as a shot of lemon or grapefruit. This will trick your mind into associating unhealthy treats with unpleasant tastes, making the impulse less appealing the next time.

The *PRS Craving Reset* effectively manages eating impulses. The more you use it, the better you will control unhealthy snacking desires.

90

Limiting Substances

Alcohol, sugar, stimulants

HEALTH

Practice Abstinence

📅 **WEEKLY**   🕐 **24 HOURS**

An unhealthy lifestyle leads to unhealthy intakes. Too much stress or too much work inevitably means too much caffeine, energy drinks, or alcohol to keep us going or entertained.

Regular rest is a must for our bodies.

With the idea that consistency beats intensity, instead of "dry January", this habit suggests a weekly abstention to safeguard your health and keep your body at rest.

Once every week, take a complete break from unhealthy intakes and replace them with healthier alternatives, as below:

Avoid	Replace with
Alcohol	Ginger Tea or sparkling water infused with citrus and mint
Caffeine	Warm lemon water or tea
Refined sugar	Fruit slices with cinnamon, banana with nut butter, or Medjool dates
Snacks	Raw nuts, hummus with carrot sticks, seaweed crisps
Energy drinks	Coconut water or electrolyte-enhanced mineral water
Heavy meals	Light veggie soup, steamed greens, or broth with herbs

Practicing such a replacement daily would be even better, but there must be a start to everything. Increase the pace over time.

Regularly engaging in such a reset improves your liver and your digestive system. It also conditioned your mind for better intake practices.

Rest & Recovery

Scheduling downtime

MOVEMENT

Stretch Your Body Every Day

📅 **DAILY**   🕐 **5 MIN**

First impressions count; we all know that. But how many of us think beyond social interactions and apply this saying to other parts of our lives?

Mornings are the first impression of your day, so treat them right to set your mind right. The better you start off your first waking hour, the better you set the tone for the rest of your day.

Use a morning stretching ritual to prime yourself for an agile, energy-driven day.

Every morning, before showering, engage in 10-minute slow body loops. Move in gentle circular motions from head to toe, utilizing neck rolls, shoulder rolls, spine twists, hip circles, and ankle rotations to stretch. Move slowly and rhythmically, letting your body follow the tempo of your breath. The movements should be fluid.

Once done, follow up with activation movements: standing up, starting with chin tucks, arm swings, and toe scrunches or heel lifts, followed by cat-cow and hip openers on a floor mat.

Starting your mornings with slow, conscious stretching exercises helps warm up your body after a night of inactivity. It also sets the tone for an empowering, successful day.

Rest & Recovery

Scheduling downtime

NUTRITION

Maintain an Evening Ritual

BI WEEKLY   **1 HOUR**

If mornings are the first impression of your day, evenings are the last and should be treated with equal care. The body's metabolism responds differently at various times of the day, so timing things correctly is crucial.

In the evening:

1. **Manage your food consumption**: Lower the intake volume and enjoy lighter and more digestion-friendly food, such as steamed or mashed vegetables or a simple broth. The body does not need a high food volume throughout the night.
2. **Manage your screen time**: Pair light meals with social presence or just silence, reinforced by a no-screen policy.
3. **Release body tension**: Lie on a mat on your back, hold your knees in a fetal position, and let your body make its own movements––left and right, back and forward––to relax your back, shoulders, and hips using your body weight.

Such a habit is a great way to lighten your body and reconnect your mind, which will also improve your quality of sleep.

93
Rest & Recovery
Scheduling downtime

HEALTH

Impose Screen Fasting Day on Yourself

📅 **WEEKLY**   🕐 **24 HOURS**

Digital devices have taken over our lives, and this book emphasizes cutting their use as much as possible. Reconnecting with yourself regularly is essential.

Once a week, go on a full-day digital fast to recalibrate your mind and reconnect with your body.

Organize an intentional program to replace it, such as the one below, and feel free to personalize it.

8:00	**Begin your day with infused water, lemon and mint, and light stretching.**
9:00	Walk, bike, or run in nature, followed by a generous, healthy breakfast.
10:00	Engage in outdoor activities such as gardening or deep breathing to further connect with nature.
12:00	Return for a mid-sized lunch with seasonal ingredients.
13:00	Take a leisurely walk or swim to digest.
14:00	Engage in a creative task to declutter your brain and rest your body, such as writing, art, or photography.
15:00	Commit to a home or family-focused activity, such as cleaning, fixing, or spending time outside with your loved ones.
17:00	Read a physical book.
19:00	End the day with a yoga session or stretching.
20:00	Dine lightly before bed.

A screen fasting routine encourages limiting screen time through an intentional program combining physical activities and recovery periods.

94

Balance & Coordination

Staying agile and body-aware

MOVEMENT

Exercise Your Balance

📅 **DAILY** 🕐 **15 MIN**

Balance is one of the abilities that comes for granted until it worsens. It is also a critical ability in almost every sport on land. Tai Chi made an art of it.

Train your balance with *stability grounding exercises*. Every day, start by standing barefoot on one leg for 2 minutes each while doing any regular task, such as cooking or, more difficultly, cleaning. Stay relaxed, engage your core, and let your stabilizer muscles do the work.

Next, stand on one foot or two feet, depending on your abilities, and begin a reactive stepping drill.

Use a shuffle playlist or an app that calls out random footwork directions (left, right, forward, etc.). Practice with concentration, keeping your movements as controlled, quick, and precise as possible.

Last, if you feel up to a challenge, stand on one foot, close your eyes, and reach your other foot slowly, forward, on the side, and backward.

The *Stability Grounding Exercises* will help you improve control of your balance and sense of space.

Balance & Coordination

Staying agile and body-aware

NUTRITION

Eat to Strengthen Your Balance

DAILY   **10 MIN**

Improving balance can also be done through food. Although there is no instant magical food for greater balance, studies show that omega-3 fatty acids support the balance function of our brains.

A suitable meal plan with food stimulating balance-related capacities can help as well.

Below are some examples of ingredients you can include in your meals:

1. A magnesium-rich source, such as pumpkin seeds or avocado, supports neuromuscular stability.
2. A source of omega-3s or anti-inflammatory ingredients such as salmon, turmeric, and berries, supporting balance-related brain function.
3. A balance-boosting smoothie with banana, avocado, blueberries, chia seed, and ginger, supporting nerves and muscles

Another way to make it easy to visualize if food is contributing to balance functions is to detect them through colors: greens (magnesium), deep blues or reds (antioxidants), and yellows/oranges (anti-inflammatory). You're probably on the right track if your plate has all three.

Remember, the key is reinforcing an essential ability, not finding a magic potion that suddenly improves it.

96
Balance & Coordination
Staying agile and body-aware

HEALTH

Exercise Movement Coordination

🗓 **DAILY**   🕐 **10 MIN**

In many sports, speed and agility often beat raw strength. Training your brain to develop capacities such as speed, agility, and balance requires specific exercises that must be practiced regularly and consistently.

This habit invites you to three distinct practices to improve your coordination and, in turn, your balance.

Every day, go through the routine below:

- Stand in front of a mirror, using both hands to "draw" a preset series of 5 symmetric movements in the air (e.g., a circle or a square), engaging both hemispheres of your brain.
- Next, repeat the same movements on paper, holding one pen in each hand.
- Then, try a brief shut-eye walk (10 steps in a hazard-free area), focusing on foot pressure and direction and aiming to reach a circle drawn on the floor.

Note the key takeaways from your performance, highlighting specific aspects, and focus on improvement.

This practice helps preserve motor control, spatial awareness, and coordination, which tend to decline with aging and certain neurological conditions.

SOCIAL

Nurture relationships in love, family, and friendship
to grow joy, trust, and lasting support.

Active Listening

Presence in conversations

LOVE

Develop Mutual Emotional Awareness

📅 **DAILY**   🕐 **1 MIN**

Successful relationships are all about communication. No matter how much you love each other, there's no simple spell that allows your partner to know how you're feeling magically. To truly feel understood, you must first help others understand.

Create a set of DIY fridge magnets representing specific emotions, such as "lonely", "hopeful", or "overwhelmed." Create two magnets for each emotion and place them in a basket or drawer that is easily accessible.

As often as you and your partner want, each of you will choose a magnet from the box and stick it on the fridge to quietly communicate your emotional state.

This is a simple tool to open to your partner without verbal communication or sending signals. Placing a magnet on the fridge is easy and non-confrontational, paving the way for open conversations.

Regularly practicing this habit allows you to better comprehend your partner's mood and how it fluctuates. It helps to get a clearer understanding of what they need and when, and this builds greater intimacy between you two, strengthening your relationship and removing misunderstandings stemming from unspoken, bottled emotions.

98

Active Listening

Presence in conversations

FAMILY

Encourage and Practice Freedom of Expression

📅 **DAILY**   🕐 **10 MIN**

Moments at home, when healthy, are perfect for growing self-confident communication: an attentive and caring audience, still offering some of the "public speaking" aspects one would face in front of a different audience.

In any relationship, being heard ranks as one of the top needs. And truly listening takes practice.

A good way to practice it at home is to ensure everyone has their 10-minute spotlight moment and your loved ones' voices aren't ignored.

Every day, one person in the household gets 10 minutes of uninterrupted speaking time to talk about whatever they want. Nobody gets to interrupt. No objections, comments, or suggestions.

The point is to create a safe listening space and allow your loved ones' voices to be recognized and truly heard. It helps them to speak up (and, therefore, grow confidence), and it helps you to listen. You may use creative cues to represent the start of this profound listening/talking moment, such as switching on a specific lamp or placing a toy microphone on the table.

In relationships, the compounding effect of healthy habits goes a long way. Allowing your loved ones to vocalize their fears, hopes, or dreams turns your home into a safe place for the people you live with and brings you closer to them.

99
Active Listening
Presence in conversations

FRIENDSHIP

Develop Active Listening

📅 **WEEKLY**   🕐 **30 MIN**

There are many aspects to listening. Sure, part of it includes hearing the other person without interrupting. But in a relationship, genuine listening goes beyond just that. It's also an active process where your loved one's voice isn't just noise in your ears. They must feel someone is genuinely listening to them.

I went to the park with my dog and ...

To practice this skill in a fun way, each of your friends narrates a story that happened to them in the past week, omitting one key detail on purpose.

All other friends' jobs are to listen attentively to the story and try to figure out the missing details by asking a maximum of three specific questions each. After the three questions, everyone gives one guess as to what was omitted in the story.

Much laughter will be guaranteed, and it encourages active listening and interest in your friends' lives. This strengthens relationships along the way and adds color to your gatherings.

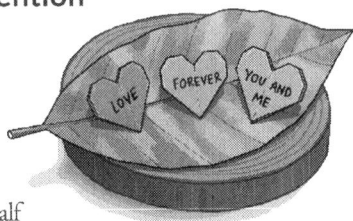

100
Kindness Rituals
Small daily acts for others

LOVE

Demonstrate Meaningful, Loving Attention

MONTHLY   **15 MIN**

One of the easiest ways to fracture a relationship is by taking it for granted. This is not an opinion; it's a fact. When you no longer put in the effort to let your other half know how special and important he or she is, that's when irreversible damage happens. So, if you want to nurture and preserve that special relationship, show your partner that you care.

While caring should be lived daily, complementing your attitude with intentional, meaningful gifts maintains a sense of "I am thinking about you".

Every month, make a meaningful display of the Art of Gifting for the attention of the person you love: a handmade creation of yours and a beautiful word painted or drawn on a natural element. To make it an "art", ensure the gift presentation stands out.

Examples to stimulate your imagination:

Create
- A hand-stitched pouch
- A custom bookmark with shared memories or the other person's favorite interest
- Tiny origami hearts – each folded heart contains a meaningful message
- A short comic with a familiar story you both cherish

Natural Element
- A Smooth River Stone – Use a metallic pen to write a powerful one-word message like *Love*, *Home*, or *Always*
- A Fallen Leaf – Carefully press and flatten it, then write a quote or phrase using a fine-tipped paint pen
- A Piece of Driftwood – Carve or paint meaningful words
- A Seashell – Write a short message inside the curve to be discovered like a secret

Presentation Magnifying
- Tighten up your gift with natural rope to hang from a branch or an indoor plant
- Placed inside a hollowed-out book wrapped with a beautiful ribbon.

You can use a thousand words or say it with one action.

138

101

Kindness Rituals

Small daily acts for others

FAMILY

Think About Others, Not Just Yourself

📅 **WEEKLY**   🕐 **1 HOUR**

Caring is often best demonstrated by small acts of kindness.

Displaying that proof of love as often as possible creates an environment where everyone cares for one another and sets new benchmarks of attention.

To stimulate this type of attention and perhaps teach the younger ones to develop that caring mindset, do the following:

Put the name of every household person in a jar, and next to it, in a different jar, include an assortment of "kind acts" written by each family member. It could be things like "Cook For Me", "Do the Dishes", "Read Me a Story", etc.

Here is the game:

Every week on Sunday, every family member draws in a quiet place, one name from the first jar and two acts of kindness from the second jar. Others should not see what you picked.

Everyone is now meant to perform the actions for the person picked up at a time of their choosing during the week. Convey love and care when you do them.

This fun family habit teaches everyone to act meaningfully for others without expecting a direct return. It's an easy and fun method for keeping relationships vibrant and filled with mutual appreciation.

102

Kindness Rituals

Small daily acts for others

FRIENDSHIP

Use Humor to Strengthen Social Connection

🗓 **WEEKLY**   🕐 **5 MIN**

How often do you think of your friends? Do you sometimes find yourself smiling privately, imagining how they might have reacted to certain situations?

Friendship is about having fun, and building habits around it is essential.

Every week, in a specific group chat, each friend could create fun memes/GIFs about one another. Memes can then be used in your regular chat when interacting.

Memes are digital, usually funny content representing someone in an unexpected situation or with a specific message.

You can effortlessly use websites like *imgflip.com* to create any meme you want. Over time, you can gather these memes in a folder to refer to them for a good laugh and to remind yourself of good memories.

This is a fun way to make fun of each other, build stronger bonds, and keep everyone connected.

103

Quality Time
Prioritizing meaningful relationships

LOVE

Disconnect to Reconnect with Others

📅 **MONTHLY**   🕐 **24 HOURS**

Here's something to ponder: When are you really with your partner? No, I don't mean watching a movie together or going shopping. I mean truly living each other's presence and switching off all the outside noise until it's just the two of you left.

Even a couple of hours of such meaningful time can strengthen your relationship.

It should expand to at least a day every month, if not every week, to truly connect with the person you love.

As publicly stated, Marc Randolph, one of *Netflix's* founders, used to block out his Tuesday evenings for dinner with his wife. It was like a ritual that nothing could disturb, and he took pride in having been married to the same woman throughout his life, unlike many of the serial entrepreneurs he knew. The Tuesday dinners were non-negotiable.

Quality time means no distractions, and the most significant distraction is technology. Make it an unplugged day, just the two of you together. Remember, the point is to be fully present, giving your partner the attentiveness and undivided attention they deserve. Make your day count with slow-down activities, such as walking, cooking, or doing something you love, allowing yourself to disconnect from the world and reconnect with those around you.

104
Quality Time
Prioritizing meaningful relationships

FAMILY

Develop the Art of Teaching

📅 **WEEKLY**   🕐 **30 MIN**

How much time do you truly spend with your family? Do you share the same space while remaining distant from each other?

This habit is an easy, fun way to reconnect with your loved ones.

Every week, one family member becomes the "Host" and teaches something to everyone else. The activity could be anything, from baking cookies, teaching salsa or fun facts, or even for your kids to teach something they learned at school. It helps them grow confidence and become accustomed to the art of teaching others.

Expertise isn't the goal; the point is to share deeper connections and bond over teaching sessions. Let love, light, and laughter lead the way, and let your home become a funhouse. You can even make the host wear a special hat or badge to add to the reality of the role. Just make sure you play with all your heart and be genuinely involved.

This is a simple, gamified way to maintain family awareness and regularly include your loved ones and connect with them.

105

Quality Time

Prioritizing meaningful relationships

FRIENDSHIP

Strengthen Friendship With 1-on-1 Meetings

📅 **MONTHLY**   🕐 **2 HOURS**

Remember the good old days of childhood? When you and your friends had all the time in the world to do whatever you wanted. Then adulthood came knocking, and suddenly, you're struggling to meet just a few times a year.

This simple habit helps you maintain friendships in a more structured way than, "I'll call you soon."

Every month, block a date for one person from your friend's group to choose three fun-filled, easy-to-plan activities, like brunch, a hike, or a game night, trying to make the event as original as possible, including at least one entirely new activity or location. No last-minute excuses whatsoever. You must show up unless it's a genuine emergency.

As a bonus, you and your friend could craft a playlist, adding songs you like before every meeting and playing them when you meet somewhere you can play music.

This habit focuses on 1-on-1 connection, privileging intimacy.

Monthly meetings around engaging activities are an effective way to keep your friends engaged intentionally. And if one of your friends can't dedicate half a day at least once every two months, they are either very poorly organized or perhaps not truly your friend.

106
Networking & Connection

Building bridges, not walls

LOVE

Socialize With Other Couples

📅 **MONTHLY**   🕐 **2 HOURS**

A couple who can't expand outside of their circle is unhealthy. It is essential to be open to the world, discover others together, and maintain a shared network. It somehow means coming together as a team.

Every month, you and your loved one, with other couples in your friend circle, can take turns organizing a "couples gathering". It could be a special-themed dinner, game night, or park picnic. The point isn't to be extravagant but to foster intentional connections, strengthen your network, and potentially involve each other's kids in the gathering with games such as Kid Olympics or drawing competitions.

Maintaining mindlike couples in your network is great for you and your partner to have common friends and socialize together. This habit also helps your couple adapt in a social context, strengthening the bonds between you two and extending the warmth of hosting. Both of you work together when being the host, which benefits your collaborative spirit as well.

107
Networking & Connection
Building bridges, not walls

FAMILY

Care for Neighborly Relationships

📅 **YEARLY**   🕐 **4 HOURS**

How welcoming your neighboring community is holds far more importance than where you live or how lavish your neighbors may be. A warm, caring circle of people living in the same vicinity can give a sense of belonging, comfort, and welcome.

In France, each year, on the last Friday of May, is Neighbors' Day. On that day, neighbors invite each other, and the tradition is that everyone brings something from home to share with others.

You could also stimulate relationships in your neighborhood by organizing a casual garden party at the early start of the summer season and inviting nearby residents to attend.

Emphasize a hearty, rustic, and casual setup of tables, music, and an open BBQ for everyone to feel welcome. This event should be less about sophistication and more about hospitality to help people connect and build meaningful relationships and for kids to connect.

The Neighbor's Party is a great way to kick off your summer on the right foot and raise your community's spirits. The onus on effort over perfection reduces unnecessary worries and turns the occasion into a joyous day for all involved.

108
Networking & Connection
Building bridges, not walls

FRIENDSHIP

Surround Yourself with Growth-Minded People

📅 **MONTHLY**   🕐 **2 HOURS**

Jim Rohn, a renowned American entrepreneur, motivational speaker, and personal development coach, once said: "You are the average of the five people you spend the most time with."

A community of people with shared interests is a hub of inspiration and innovation, and it must be a community pushing everyone towards greater success.

If you're having trouble finding a community like this, you can create one yourself. The Business Circle +1 helps you develop this idea.

Start with 3 to 4 friends or acquaintances who share similar interests, such as entrepreneurship, a sport you are interested in, or something else.

Host a monthly meeting with a light structure where everyone can connect and discuss new ideas, inspirational topics, and any point of interest. Emphasize growth and learning over idle chitchat.

Now, here's the twist: Every month, every club member should bring along a new member. This keeps the gathering informative and your circle growing. Over time, it transforms it into a dynamic, thriving community of like-minded people.

Priming your social circle for monthly motivation and interesting discussions is excellent for expanding your horizons and developing a growing mindset. It also keeps you aware of new trends and different approaches.

109

Support Systems

Knowing when and how to lean

LOVE

Exercise Emotional Intelligence

📅 **WEEKLY**   🕐 **30 MIN**

It can't be said enough: A healthy relationship is about listening, understanding, and supporting, which are some of the strongest foundations and meanings of love.

A playful way to cultivate those essential aspects of love is to be aware of each other's needs and help both of you delve into your partner's psyche and understand their feelings.

Every week, each partner creates three decks of three different colors each. Each card in the deck contains self-written prompts based on three themes:

- *Daily Life, representing things you or your partner want to see more of, or less of, in your daily life, living together*
- *Common Projects, representing needs and wishes relating to common projects*
- *Feelings, representing feelings towards each other*

The decks are placed conveniently for the other partner to access them (e.g., your partner's decks may be placed on your desk).

Every week, each partner draws one card from the other partner's deck and reads the prompt by themselves. Each partner can ask any question 24 hours after reading, which is the minimum time to process new information with enough maturity. The decks are updated monthly with new cards or by removing existing cards.

Sometimes, it can be hard to let go of what's inside you and share your vulnerability with someone else. The fun approach lightens this by easing the message sharing and allowing everyone to think about important things for each partner while keeping the process fun and engaging.

This habit helps deepen relationships and be aware of the other partner's needs on a recurring basis, without having to guess them.

110
Support Systems
Knowing when and how to lean

FAMILY

Set Healthy Boundaries

⊞ **WEEKLY**   🕐 **1 DAY**

As much as human presence and support is nice, silence, self-reflection, and moments of solitude are equally crucial for the well-being of anyone's mind. Making space in your life for such moments plays a key role in maintaining healthy relationships.

Having ways to draw healthy boundaries helps communicate these needs, and this is what this habit is about.

First, create small magnets for every family member labelled with everyday private needs or areas where they do not need help. These magnets are kept in each family member's bedroom and put on a metallic board hung on each family member's bedroom door to communicate these needs for autonomy.

The token labels can include:

- Private Time
- Meditation Session Ongoing
- Need for Concentration
- Sensitive Weeks Ahead

The rest of the household must respect these needs, which can be updated weekly. Think of the token instructions as a gentle way to communicate your need for privacy and for you to respect the needs of others.

Contrary to most people's belief, such ways do not create distance among family members; they bring people closer because everyone gets the freedom they need. As these needs get respected, your home naturally becomes a space with fewer conflicts. Boundaries are healthy in any relationship.

111

Support Systems
Knowing when and how to lean

FRIENDSHIP

Use Your Network to Support Your Life

📅 **QUARTERLY**   🕐 **30 MIN**

Think of yourself as part of a team comprising all the people you can rely on in your life. Being surrounded by people with skills different from yours and who can help you is an excellent hack for growth, support, and success.

As much as you should make your expertise and time available to others, it is incredible to know that you can benefit from others' knowledge and time. Knowing who you can turn to and who you should support takes all its importance from there.

This habit is about formalizing and using this awareness to help your social circle to your most significant advantage.

Create a two-column list, with the first column titled "Who I Can Lean on" and "Who Might Need Me".

Next, create four rows titled:

⏰ Time

💪 Physical Activities

💬 Emotional Support

💼 Professional Support

Fill in each row with specific names of people within your social circle. Update this list every 3 months, and feel free to add sub-rows and additional areas where support may be needed.

This is a great way to constantly ensure you have the support you need and that you can give back to others.

112

Conflict Management

Emotional maturity

LOVE

Develop a Conflict No-Go List

📅 **DAILY**　🕐 **5 MIN**

Having conflictual interactions is one thing, and knowing how to handle them is another. Approaching challenging interactions with a level of detachment and maturity can often be helpful.

Avoiding the "red line" is crucial because once it is crossed, it becomes harder to restore the relationship to a safe zone, which can lead to irreversible damage.

While every situation is different, there are standard practices to prevent things from spiraling out of hand. To help you avoid making usual mistakes, the most important attitudes to prevent them are listed below:

- **Mocking or sarcasm**. Erodes trust and makes your partner feel belittled.
- **Interrupting or raising your voice**. Escalates tension and shuts down healthy communication.
- **Bringing up past unrelated issues**. Distracts from the current issue and adds more complexity to solving the problem.
- **Silent treatment or dramatic exits**. Blocks resolution and creates emotional distance.
- **Using "always" or "never" language**. Exaggerates faults and feels accusatory, not constructive.
- **Threatening to leave or withdrawing love**. Instills fear and damages the foundation of the relationship.

The list should be written down and easily accessible so you can read it daily and remove these types of reactions from your attitude in conflictual times.

Making a situation worse is never helpful, regardless of your frustration. If you genuinely care about the relationship with the person you are engaged in a conflict with, or for what the situation involves, be as constructive and mature as possible.

113

Conflict Management

Emotional maturity

FAMILY

Develop Emotional Maturity

DAILY   **2 DAYS**

As words carry much weight, an unchecked tongue can cause much harm. Just one moment of blind rage is all it takes to do or say something that can never be taken back and, in some situations, something that you will never be able to make up for.

To avoid living with regrets over impulsive reactions and words that you didn't mean, building self-control is easier said than done.

A couple of rules can help you develop Emotional Maturity if you follow them.

1. **Never write about your frustrations**; instead, discuss them. Spoken words are fleeting, and written words endure.
2. **Pause before reacting**. If you feel a situation getting out of hand, removing yourself to come back with a clearer mind is the best way to handle it, 99% of the time.
3. **Speak in "I"**. Use "I feel..." instead of "You always..." It avoids making the other person feel accused.
4. **Reformulate what you hear before responding**. It shows active listening and mutual understanding.
5. **Return to the situation with a resolution**. When you return to the discussion, prepare a thoughtful resolution focused on the impact without carrying an emotional charge. Avoid the "It was my fault, but..." It reopens conflicts.

It's impossible to think clearly when you're emotionally overwhelmed.

Emotional maturity is a skill, and it often means setting aside one's ego, avoiding personal victory, and privileging mutual resolution instead.

114

Conflict Management

Emotional maturity

FRIENDSHIP

Don't Weight Yourself With Passive Resentments

QUARTERLY   **30 MIN**

Resentment is like a plague: if you keep ignoring it, it will quietly spread until the relationships are poisoned completely, beyond the point of saving.

Everyone has already encountered such ill feelings, and opening up to address their roots is the only way to develop healthier relationships.

Every quarter, engage in an introspective session and unveil potentially hidden resentments you're hiding within. If you can think of such feelings, it's time to resolve them instead of keeping them a secret. Here are some points to keep in mind for the resolution:

- **Prioritize face-to-face interactions**, as they allow for direct connection and a greater understanding.
- **Introduce the issue with tact** rather than presenting it with drama and seriousness.
- **Choose your words wisely**. Avoid antagonizing and focus on gaining the other person's understanding.
- **Be open to the possibility of any explanations**, and don't shy away from accepting responsibility where you've made an error.
- **Always end such interactions on a light note** to eliminate awkwardness and emphasize that your shared relationship is more important than the potential issue.

These are practical advice to clear relationship misunderstandings rather than silently suffering them.

The more you care about the foundations of your relationships, the greater the quality of your relationships is.

Mentorship & Giving Back

Sharing wisdom

LOVE

Invest in Growing People Around You

📅 **MONTHLY**   🕐 **15 MIN**

Growing together is one of the best aspects of love.

And sometimes, the old ways are the best when it comes to love. They possess a soul that the modern tech-obsessed era lacks and can never compensate for.

Every month, offer the person you love a way for him or her to develop meaningfully: a book, an audiobook, an online course, or a masterclass, for example. Include your gift in an envelope (or the envelope in the book, in case of a book) and write a short note to explain why you chose this training or book. It adds even more weight to your present and helps make it feel even more purposeful.

Helping someone reach their highest potential is extremely meaningful, and developing such a gesture into a habit doesn't cost much but can have a lasting impact.

Showing unshakable belief in your partner through commitment to their development is proof of love, greater than 1,000 words!

116

Mentorship & Giving Back

Sharing wisdom

FAMILY

Connect With Other Generations to Keep Learning

📅 MONTHLY   🕐 15 MIN

The younger and older generations lived in vastly different worlds, making connections sometimes difficult. The younger generation tends to feel the older generation is entitled, while the older generation tends to feel the younger generation is inexperienced.

However, while it can often be a source of difference and misunderstanding, it can also be an extremely powerful force if the two can connect. The key is connecting and stimulating a shift of perspective from both sides.

When have you truly practiced nurturing such a connection?

Build a ritual with someone from your family and of a different generation where you and another family member sit down for a heart-to-heart learning session every month.

During the session, every person involved has 15 minutes of free speech, and the same person is allowed up to three questions to be answered that time, by others people. Time can be expanded if so required, of course.

Your "free speech" moments can be made of anything, from a poignant childhood story, an incident from the past, or even a current trend.

The main focus should be on keeping an open mind and being receptive to the knowledge coming your way, no matter how strong your opinion may be.

To add meaning, make it a ritual by meeting at the same place and time. Over time, this will deepen your relationship and help both generations understand each other and keep an open mind.

117

Mentorship & Giving Back

Sharing wisdom

FRIENDSHIP

Use Your Social Circle to Develop Yourself

MONTHLY   **30 MIN**

Friendship can help elevate us, so it's essential to choose our surroundings wisely. Engaging with friends in meaningful ways is also a great way to grow.

Develop a ritual to meet once a month with a chosen friend over a learning session, with the following structure:

1. Both of you share a book you recently loved, explain why, and lend it to each other.
2. Both of you share an audiobook or podcast that deeply impacted you. It can also be a short video. Again, the point is to explain why.
3. Both of you review the previous book and audiobook shared during the last session and explain if you liked it or not and why.
4. Both of you share one significant life path you're exploring or a fundamental principle you have included.

This locks you and your friend into a cycle of mutual enrichment, with a halo effect, where you both trade points of view and wisdom and keep pushing each other up the ladder of life understanding.

Community Participation

Being part of something bigger

LOVE

Give Back Using Your Skills

📅 **WEEKLY**   🕐 **2 HOURS**

Aside from our love for each other, a shared purpose is a great way to connect two people. It hides differences and emphasizes the understanding of one another in the process. And the purpose does not have to be financially related, either.

Commit to building your co-founded charity relying on the skills you both possess. Every week, dedicate two hours where you and your partner work on a cause larger than yourselves and experience the joy of giving together.

You can offer design services to non-profit organizations, co-host wellness sessions, create content to raise awareness, or support others through your skills, positively influencing the world around you.

To keep things up and have a broader impact on your actions, you can even invite other couples to join you in the effort, further solidifying the cause you support.

The point is to focus on impact, no matter how small, and be drawn together for a united purpose. Keeping things non-financially related fosters a mutual understanding of the other person and low pressure. It builds appreciation for their role in the shared venture, which inevitably reflects in your relationship.

Community Participation

Being part of something bigger

FAMILY

Cultivate Healthy Values

📅 **QUARTERLY**   🕐 **1 DAY**

A group is only as strong as its weakest link. The same holds for a family. If you want your relationships to thrive, you must ensure that you and your loved ones share the same values. And this habit helps you build this shared unity.

After all, building healthy values is even better when done early and as a family.

Every quarter, commit your family to a collective community project that positively impacts your neighborhood, such as building a public library, planting a neighborhood herb garden, or assembling care kits for a local shelter.

Everyone in the family should participate, from the youngest to the oldest, with roles fitting their abilities. It ensures every family member is involved in making a difference and developing team spirit among family members.

To add to the ritual, ensure the initiative is followed by a nice lunch or dinner to celebrate the achievement.

Families that work together stay together. Regularly working on a good cause for the benefit of your neighborhood is a great way to build and maintain family values and ensure that family members learn the impact of proximity care.

120
Community Participation
Being part of something bigger

FRIENDSHIP

Contribute Meaningfully to Benefit the Local Community

QUARTERLY   **4 HOURS**

All human beings, no matter who they are, have a creative element within them. Exercising creativity benefits our souls, fills us with purpose, and can also help others and impact the world, which is fantastic.

Gather some friends and commit your creative talents to positively impact your local community, relying on existing artistic skills or developing new ones.

An artistically diverse range of possibilities could be developed, such as:

- Co-creating murals or quilts with a collective canvas project
- Recording community stories, creating a storytelling booth
- Offering free portraits to those in need
- Host cause-driven screenings with community film nights
- Create free art workshops to allow others to express themselves through painting, for example.

Creativity, Community, and Charity are the three pillars of this habit to implement once per quarter, inspiring you and your friends into better versions of themselves and being connected through a meaningful cause involving art.

Regular activities of this type deepen friendships and help you connect with the local community.

PASSION

Pursue your passions through curiosity, practice,
and growth to feel alive and fulfilled.

Creative Expression

Art, writing, music, or building

EXPLORATION

Remain Curious About New Hobbies

MONTHLY **1 HOUR**

If you struggle to know yourself and understand who you truly are, it might be time to explore new hobbies and art. Walking untrodden paths and trying out new avenues is how you discover hidden passions and strengths within you. Hobbies have enough low pressure to make you feel relaxed and still enough intensity for you to feel truly involved.

Making it a regular ritual of self-discovery and exploring a new hobby every month can be a good way to naturally discover different interests, which can later develop into new passions.

Every month, choose an unfamiliar hobby on platforms like *YouTube*, *Domestika*, or *Skillshare*. Explore it without any underlying pressure to achieve mastery. Whether you choose word poetry, clay modeling, or shadow puppetry is up to you. The endeavor must intrigue you and incite your curiosity.

Doing it yourself can be a first step, but this habit could become even more concrete if you commit to publishing your work on your YouTube channel, for example, engaging your audience at the same time!

Remember that the goal is to stimulate curiosity and inspire exploration, not to turn it into a race toward perfection. This habit aims to stimulate curiosity and discovery, with an optional added perk: engaging an audience in sharing discoveries, which can make it even more fun.

122
Creative Expression
Art, writing, music, or building

PRACTICE

Commit to Repetitive Free Expression

MONTHLY   **4 DAYS**

Human beings' greatest power is creativity. It makes life worth living and fills our days with purpose, and to avoid losing it, we must exercise it regularly.

This time, it is not about diversity but commitment, sticking to one hobby and aiming for a minimum volume to impregnate your craft with better execution over time.

Every month, make it a point to create 100 imperfect creative exhibits focusing on one creative hobby. Prioritizing regular practice over perfection, you could, for example, create handmade zines, narrated photo albums, poetry decks, or even podcast episodes. It's up to you.

The production pressure should remain low while the necessity to "get going" remains. It helps you overcome perfection and celebrate continuous progress, motivating you even more. Inevitably, the more you practice, the better your creative abilities get, and your confidence develops.

This habit helps with using creative hobbies as an engaging and fun way to commit to consistency, fostering discipline and widening your perspective, allowing you to broaden the range of possibilities.

Creative Expression

Art, writing, music, or building

DEVELOPMENT

Develop a Growth Mindset in Creativity

📅 **DAILY**　　🕐 **10 MIN**

As empowering as creative endeavors are, they may sometimes feel intimidating or discouraging along the way. Writing a book, for example, can be daunting when staring at an empty page. As a result, most people choose to avoid creativity simply because of how intimidating it seems.

Developing a growth mindset in creativity can be hacked through a couple of good practices, which are listed here:

1. **Keep your draft**. Photograph earlier drafts to compare with final versions and have concrete proof of your progress.
2. **Consider any complete work at approximately 70%** and return to it only later. This overcomes perfectionism barriers and maintains momentum.
3. **Gather valuable opinions from a self-elected "review committee"**. Share your finished pieces with a selected number of people and ask them to share an honest opinion. Accept their point of view and perfect your craft.
4. **Create a "failure wall"**, celebrating your boldest or most ambitious attempts that didn't pan out. This will stimulate excellence.
5. **Store unfinished projects** in a folder to revisit them in a year. This prevents a failure mindset and turns an unfinished project into a work-in-progress.

Mastering your craft can be challenging, but if you consistently follow these five rules, you will cultivate a growth mindset, which can help you navigate the hardships involved.

124

Self-Discovery

Understanding your unique identity and needs

EXPLORATION

Start Small at Low-Stakes

📅 **MONTHLY**   🕐 **30 MIN**

Richard Branson, the founder of the Virgin Group, is well known for his lean and experimental approach to business. One of the beliefs he regularly advocated for is that if you can't make it work on a small scale within a few weeks, it will probably not work at all.

This type of approach could easily be incorporated into your life as well. Every month, pick a low-stakes side experiment, a curious idea you've always wanted to try, and try it, whether it be creating a fake product page, writing a mini e-book, testing a small podcast concept, or building a website, taking that tiny first step forward towards the idea's completion.

The rules to follow are:

1. Keep the scope narrowed; focus on one product only
2. Test it over 2 weeks only, and see if there is any interest
3. Act quickly, then adjust

Remember, the goal isn't perfection; it is to try your initiative on a small scale before dedicating serious resources and being less worried about risks.

Taking risks should never be a strategy; however, taking calculated risks is often a key factor in achieving project success.

125

Self-Discovery

Understanding your unique identity and needs

PRACTICE

Collect Inspiring Samples

📅 **DAILY**   🕐 **30 MIN**

To stimulate new ideas and be creative, you must inspire your mind. A little bit like a plant, you keep watering daily to develop its roots and flowers. Collecting work samples that inspire you is a good way to do this, and inspiration can be present in anything: a leaf, a stone, or an advertising poster.

Every week, stay aware, pick small, preferably non-digital, items that inspire you, and add them to your "Inspiration Board". Fabric scraps, menu typographies, or magazine snippets are all examples of items you could collect.

Over time, your wall will become a tactile repository of inspiration and emotionally resonant materials. Think of it as food for your soul and something you can look at when you need inspiration.

Sometimes, big projects are born from small ideas. Approaching work with initial ideas can make a difference and unlock situations where you don't know where to start. It also influences your environment, and therefore your mind, to think creatively.

It should develop into an unending supply of inspiration by your side, empowering you to create more often and better.

126

Self-Discovery

Understanding your unique identity and needs

DEVELOPMENT

Stay Close to Who You Are

📅 **MONTHLY**　　🕐 **10 MIN**

Most of what we "are" exists in our subconscious, beyond the reach of awareness. This part of us determines our personality, emotional patterns, and behaviors. If we want to live well, we must first know ourselves.

Curate a small shelf near your creative space and add 3 to 5 objects to reflect who you are. The items could be anything, as long as they hold some symbolic value relating to your life path, whether that value is a favorite quote, a childhood photo, or a specific item. They should remind you of how you see yourself and what you do in your life to make it meaningful.

The shelf should be a symbolic display of your nature. Of course, nature will evolve as time passes, and you can keep updating your shelf each month to reflect those changes.

This habit helps you stay close to your identity, customizing your environment to keep you focused.

The closer we are to ourselves, the more we can control our lives, and the easier we can sail through difficult times, maintaining that vital inner connection and nurturing self-awareness.

127
Playfulness
Doing things for fun and joy

EXPLORATION

Be Curious About Unusual Creative Hobbies

📅 **MONTHLY**   🕐 **15 MIN**

Living a happy life involves keeping it playful. This means playing with absolute involvement but not letting the outcome affect you too much. A nifty strategy because you can dedicate yourself fully without worrying too much about potential adverse effects.

Approaching unusual creative activities is not dissimilar: You get to try your hand without knowing if you will like it, but the experience is still worth it.

Each month, pick one quirky, fun-filled hobby and try it out. Examples of lighthearted and extraordinary activities to try could be:

- Moss Art & Kokedama: Using the beauty of moss to craft living, breathing décor in transparent bowls.
- Gelli Plate Printing: Using gel textures to create layered prints.
- Resin Art Trinkets: This involves pouring colorful resin into tiny treasures.
- ASMR Crafting Videos: Making soothing sounds by engaging in therapeutic handmade creations.
- DIY Kawaii Stationery: Creating cute, customized paper supplies.
- Miniature World Building: This involves creating detailed, imaginary worlds as you please.
- Upcycling Oddities: Turning eccentric junk into quirky creations.
- Sensory Scent Blending: Mixing fragrances to spark vivid feelings.
- Food Sculpting & Character Bento Boxes: Creating aesthetic meals in a creative style.

You can even document your progress and share it on YouTube or TikTok for video format content, Pinterest for pictures, or Substack for storytelling.

128

Playfulness

Doing things for fun and joy

PRACTICE

Develop Self-Confidence Through Performances

MONTHLY   **1 HOUR**

A timeless hack for living a happy life is to be yourself unapologetically. People who fail at this often worry about what others may think, while self-confidence remains buried inside themselves.

A way to develop the concepts of being yourself and self-confident is not taking yourself too seriously and connecting with your true inner self.

To involve your family and perhaps teach your kids to develop such skills, invite everyone to participate in a silly performance night, where everyone will perform, one at a time, absurdly on stage.

To get everyone going, here are some inspirations:

- Sing a song with exaggerated gestures
- Lip-sync dramatically
- Deliver a fake TED Talk about a funny topic
- Do celebrity imitations with painful gusto
- Re-enact cringy TikTok trends
- Perform theatrical readings of hilarious texts

This is a night where you practice being yourself and letting go of all unnecessary, sophisticated ways to present yourself. Have a blast, laugh your lungs out, and make it a night to remember.

Understand: We are what we regularly practice. Exercising the most essential behaviors does not always have to be so serious or practiced in a formal environment.

Whatever is taught early instills your personality even more, so it's all the better for the younger generation.

129
Playfulness
Doing things for fun and joy

DEVELOPMENT

Play Board Games to Exercise Your Brain

📅 **WEEKLY**   🕐 **1 HOUR**

People often stress the importance of working out daily to keep the body healthy, but not many things are done to treat their brain with the same care. After all, your brain is your body's command center and deserves just as much attention, if not more.

It is recognized that playing board games has a range of advantages for the brain, including improving concentration, strategic thinking, problem-solving, memory, and social skills when playing board games with others. Not to mention that you finally get disconnected from the screens, which is never bad.

Every week, give your brain the exercise it deserves by playing a board game, either with others or solo (there are a thousand amazing solo board games.)

Many board game types exist, and below are some of the most recognized names in their genre:

- **Economic Game**: Terraforming Mars
- **Solo Game**: Tainted Grail: The Fall of Avalon
- **Fun Game**: Just One
- **Deep Thinking Game**: Brass: Birmingham
- **Card Game**: Ark Nova

Board games are like therapy. You get to play with complete involvement, letting your mind temporarily disconnect, which gives your brain the reset it needs to function at its best.

130
Vision Crafting
Dreaming big with clarity

EXPLORATION

Run Idea Incubator Sessions

📅 **WEEKLY**   🕐 **30 MIN**

Opportunity doesn't knock; it is about being curious and inspired. Therefore, cultivating curiosity and inspiration should be prioritized to encourage opportunities. However, idea collection is only one part of the opportunity-taking process; what you do with these ideas matters just as much.

After collecting ideas on an *Inspiration Board,* set aside time each week to choose one concept you've encountered, big or small, and give it a mini "incubation cycle."

Use a notebook, sketchpad, or digital tools to explore the idea with focused curiosity, asking yourself:

1. What attracted me to this idea?
2. How can I twist it to make it my own?
3. Do I have an unfair advantage? Consider any skills or interests you already possess that most people don't.
4. What's one step I can take this week to play with it?
5. How can I test this idea on a budget?

Dedicate a creative space for answering such questions, and don't hesitate to sketch and represent your ideas in the most visual ways to keep brainstorming exercises efficient.

Over time, this becomes a playground for developing ideas, where raw ideas are nurtured into something tangible. Even the wildest thoughts can become future projects, businesses, or solutions when given this focused attention.

This habit develops the capacity to act on creative ideas and develop ways to get started.

131

Vision Crafting

Dreaming big with clarity

PRACTICE

Model Ideas Before Executing Them

📅 **MONTHLY** 🕐 **30 MIN**

One small action will always be better than a thousand intentions. It's that simple. Overthinking things leads nowhere; it is about trying and trying again until it works.

A simple way to overcome hesitations is to stop focusing on the end goal and instead focus on the next small step you can take to drive things forward and take that step. This way, you create momentum, which you can use to lead to a second small step and another one. That's already three, and it is better than none!

Every month, pick one of your dream projects that may have come from your *Inspiration Board* and should have gone through your Idea Incubator process. It may be writing a book, creating a workshop, or a creative event. Whatever it is, focus on creating a playful preview of it.

This could mean designing a poster, creating a tagline, or creating a temporary landing page. The point is to take that first small step and build momentum. From there, try to "test for cheap" the client's product, service, or experience, involving family or friends.

Ideas should lead to planning. Planning should lead to action. Action eliminates doubt and facilitates further actions. The more you act, the more you'll be able to act. Keep going, and soon, your project will look more than an idea and start to make sense.

Practice it with discipline, even on ideas that feel less meaningful. Accumulating small steps leads to big leaps.

132

Vision Crafting

Dreaming big with clarity

DEVELOPMENT

Use Reverse Thinking in Project Planning

📅 **DAILY** 🕐 **2 HOURS**

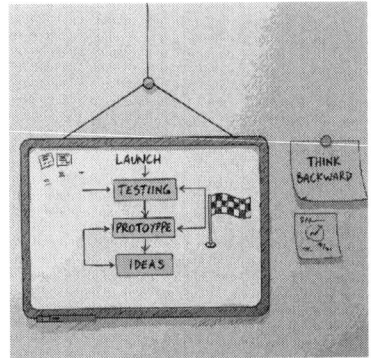

Every impossible achievement begins with a simple belief that it can be done. With unwavering faith, human beings have performed miracles on this planet, leaving no doubt that one's mindset and attitude play a pivotal role in success.

There are three ways to set up an effective plan:

1. **Start from the beginning**: Define the first step and outline each following step leading to your goal.
2. **Start from both ends**: Define the goal and the first step, then fill in the steps in between.
3. **Work backward**: Define the goal and reverse-engineer the process back to the very first actionable step.

Is there a better method than the other? Not necessarily; it is situational.

The third method is interesting and is usually less commonly used. Instead of laying out your plans from your present situation to your goal, you lay out your goal and end up back where you should start.

What are the advantages of this method?

Starting with the desired outcome makes the thinking process naturally strategic; it adds clarity due to the reverse-engineering nature of the process and reduces the overwhelming thinking process of the other methods.

This habit allows your creativity to remain grounded and achievable, motivating you to take action and inevitably resulting in visible progress.

133
Creative Expression

Making space to express yourself freely

EXPLORATION

Nurture Instinctive Creativity

📅 **DAILY**   🕐 **15 MIN**

If you're one of those people who keep waiting for inspiration to strike them, you may be waiting forever. Creativity doesn't work that way. Like any other skill, it must be regularly exercised to reach its full potential.

Nurturing instinctive creativity stimulates creative momentum and keeps your inspiration alive. When you feel stuck or lacking inspiration, try the following unlocking activities:

1. **Freestyle Creative Session:** Engage in a 10-minute unstructured creative session, utilizing any medium to express creativity most instinctively, disregarding the importance of the result.
2. **Inspired Session:** Collect random objects around you and create around them. For example, a childhood photo, writing a short, nostalgic piece on the simplicity of earlier times, or a beautiful shell collected at the beach, engaging in magnifying it through photography.

Creativity will flow through whatever channel you provide it with. Rather than waiting, take the first step and open yourself up in any way possible.

Instinctive expression is often the voice of the heart!

134
Creative Expression
Making space to express yourself freely

PRACTICE

Use Focus to Create

MONTHLY   **15 MIN**

Thinking outside the box can be very useful, but following a specific structure also has its advantages. And if you can join the two together, you have the perfect recipe for efficient progress.

Harness focused creativity to leverage this power pair and refine your craft. The two methods below draw inspiration from this approach.

1. Every month, choose one creative prompt or challenge and complete it consistently, adding a new twist each day. This could involve adding a slight variation to the prompt, utilizing a new tool, or introducing different constraints. It could, for example, be drawing a tree. Then, I will draw a tree during autumn or make a tree using a collage.

2. Use the same creative medium during a month, such as watercolor, typewriter, or mold, and practice within that single form to build a style around the chosen medium. This way, you create around a single theme, using a single medium.

Focus channels your creativity with discipline and a sense of repetition with variables to emphasize a specific style in your craft and develop uniqueness.

Focus and variation ensure you don't lose interest while compounding experience and skill.

135

Creative Expression

Making space to express yourself freely

DEVELOPMENT

Model Successful People to Find Your Own Style

📅 **MONTHLY**   🕐 **1 HOUR**

When facing tough times, remember that you're not alone. Others before you have walked the same road, failing probably even more than you, learning from their mistakes each time, and staying motivated, inspired, and determined despite all the failures. This is the winner's mindset you should have.

Modeling successful people helps you learn from the best and learn recognized methods and styles.

Every month, pick a different creator, artist, writer, or musician recognized for their accomplishments. Study them inside out, starting with their history, then their craft, the method they use, and the principles and attitudes they apply to be so successful. Watch interviews, read books, and use other media to learn as much as possible.

Once you feel you have a grasp of their ways, try them. Create small pieces of art inspired by their work. Do not copy them, but inspire your work from theirs. Your job must not be perfect; it must reflect the modeled artist's style and still have your touch.

To embody greatness, you first must know what greatness looks like, and the lives of accomplished creators offer the perfect blueprint from which to draw knowledge.

The better you understand them, the more inspired you will be to develop a style of your own, which is likely to result in similar outcomes.

Flow Activities

Doing what absorbs you so profoundly that you lose track of time

EXPLORATION

Reconnect With Childhood Passions

📅 **QUARTERLY**   🕐 **1 HOUR**

Being happy often means being focused on one activity that keeps you focused and passionate. During childhood, playfulness was the only "rule", and you were free to play; the hobbies you used to love were often your favorite for a reason. Either because they were deeply connected with you, or allowed you to express yourself freely.

Think about those special moments you experienced as a kid when time seemed to stop, immersing you in simple joy.

Deep inside, reconnect with yourself as a child and list what you used to play with, as well as anything that comes to mind. It could be games, sports, or artistic activities.

Out of the list, pick an activity and reconnect with this activity in some shape or form. For example, you may have liked trucks and cars, and although you may have outgrown playing with such toys, this theme may still interest you. Sports activities could be another example. Perhaps dance was your thing, and due to entering adulthood, you dropped it altogether.

When your mind is emptied of thoughts, and you move by pure instinct alone, focusing solely on the activity at hand, we call that state a flow state.

Productivity and creativity are highest in such a state, not to mention enthusiasm levels and attention. The more frequently you can enter a flow state, the happier your life becomes.

Choose one activity quarterly and try it again; see how happy you feel.

137

Flow Activities

Doing what absorbs you so profoundly that you lose track of time

PRACTICE

Allow Curiosity to Lead Learning

WEEKLY   **10 MIN**

The world's mysteries are endless and ever-evolving. So, if life ever feels boring, it's often because you're not exploring enough, and wonders are often much closer than we tend to think. It is just about making the effort to look.

Every week, pick an item that interests you, whether an article, video, or podcast. Whatever you want to learn from. Study the material and identify one related idea or detail in that information that further sparks your curiosity, schedule the learning of it, and do the same again with this new piece of knowledge, just like an infinite learning circle.

Keep following the crumbs, moving from one lead to the next, letting curiosity guide you and reveal more with every step.

This is good practice for instilling a natural inclination to explore and cultivate curiosity, fostering a genuine wonder for the world, which grows as you continue learning.

This is a great way to remain open and feed curiosity for growing knowledge and the universe surrounding you. Giving in to the desire to explore only strengthens them and breeds even more curiosity, opening you up to unexpected knowledge that you can gain from.

138

Flow Activities

Doing what absorbs you so profoundly that you lose track of time

DEVELOPMENT

Trick Your Brain for Creative Efficiency

⛏ **DAILY**   🕐 **15 MIN**

Flow states are truly magical if you can achieve them. They compound productivity to unparalleled heights and flood you with creative inspiration.

Tricking your brain can help you achieve a regular flow state. At your usual working or creative space, customize it for super-focus, setting up the environment to trick your mind and be at your best to create, magnifying it around the five senses:

- Emphasis on visual elements to "set the scene", such as the *Inspiration Board* we proposed in one of the earlier habits, where you collect inspiration. Or simply related tools to display your art.
- Set up a sound system and playlist that inspires you. It can be music you like or ambient and instrumental songs for deep immersion.
- Assign a unique flavor to each creative phase to build a subconscious link between flavor and focus over time. For example, Mint tea for brainstorming, Dark chocolate for refining, or Citrus water for energetic bursts.
- Prepare a rotating jar of flavored snacks or herbal teas chosen for their mood association, such as lavender for relaxation, ginger for focus, or rosemary for mental clarity.
- Set up a voice recording app or smart assistant nearby. Speak your thoughts freely before writing to help with ideas and avoid overthinking.

Your workspace should be designed to cut off outside distractions and let your creative task receive all your brain power.

Remember, the environment can trick your mind and steer you in specific directions. Use it to your advantage.

139

Passion Sharing

Inspiring others by sharing what excites and energizes you

EXPLORATION

Create a Feedback Circle

📅 **DAILY**   🕐 **15 MIN**

Feedback is a gift that allows us to see ourselves from the outside. Yet, most people hate receiving it. What's even more curious is that the feedback that hurts the most is often the very thing that could have the most positive impact on our lives and help us grow as human beings. Why not take advantage of the power of feedback and set your ego aside?

Opening up your work and creations to others takes all their meaning. Because everyone may have a different point of view, it is not only essential to gather a selected committee able to share valuable opinions, but it is also crucial to choose who should be part of this informal committee. Hence, the opinions come from specific populations of individuals.

The individual population can be chosen based on any aspect that makes an individual unique, such as Gender, Age, Origin, Culture, Skills, or Interests. The list is exhaustive, and the point is to ensure a feedback circle that can provide valuable perspectives based on what you create and your target audience.

While it is up to you to choose who should be part of your feedback circle, a good benchmark for it to be efficient is to ensure it is at least spread across age and experience levels.

It could, for example, be a child, a curious friend, and an expert whom you can consult daily.

Diverse perspectives on your creative endeavors will offer multiple angles and opinions, which you can use to assess the quality of your work.

As you incorporate the feedback where needed, you'll gain an intuitive sense of what may work and what is likely to fail, and anticipate challenges accordingly.

Passion Sharing

Inspiring others by sharing what excites and energizes you

PRACTICE

Document and Share Your Learning Process

📅 DAILY　　**🕐 30 MIN**

The road to success is always a challenging one, but walking with others makes the journey just a bit more bearable. If you have a supportive community behind you, the efforts will suddenly feel much easier, and the challenges will be less heavy. Even just for the fun of it, taking people on your trying journey is a good idea.

As you embark on your learning journey, consider using a platform like *YouTube* to share your creative journey honestly with the world. Document what you're working on, your challenges, and what you look forward to. Show your audience. Carry them on the same journey with you. Emphasize sincerity and simplicity to make them feel they are in your seat. Viewers love such content, which helps develop a healthy audience base.

Not only will you feel supported, but as you grow and become more experienced, you will have tangible proof for beginners that you were once in their shoes. And one day, you may teach others through courses or a coaching program; who knows?

Sharing is indeed caring and usually means much in return.

141

Passion Sharing

Inspiring others by sharing what excites and energizes you

DEVELOPMENT

Teach What You Love

📅 **MONTHLY**   🕐 **15 MIN**

Giving often leads to receiving in return, and the proverb "what goes around comes around" encapsulates this idea very well. It is interesting to realize that the benefits serve both the receiver and the giver.

Teaching, for example, is an act of giving, but the benefits expand beyond just the learning made by the receivers. Teachers will develop the ability to communicate, influence, and persuade their audience by receiving questions and feedback on the concepts presented in the lessons.

Every week, commit to teaching one skill, preferably along a common theme, through a short written post, video demo, or even just a conversation, and share one technique, insight, or trick in your chosen craft with the rest of the world. To achieve this reach, utilize platforms such as *Udemy*, *Teachable*, or *YouTube*, among others.

This personal challenge, coupled with the commitment to weekly publication, not only grows teaching skills but also forces you to expand your craft beyond your social circle and yourself.

Practicing teaching around topics you love and publishing courses publicly is an excellent exercise to monetize your activities if you ever decide to do so for a fee. Even if you do it for free, sharing with others carries all the above benefits and helps fuel your passion.

Passion Rituals

Creating recurring moments that keep your passion alive

EXPLORATION

Diversify Your Environment to Create

WEEKLY   **90 MIN**

Your environment conditions your mind to think in specific ways, and if you feel stuck creatively, it may be time to change your surroundings. Creating in the same place is likely to mean thinking and acting the same way, being drawn by the same inspiration, and resulting in the same things.

For a recurring creative activity, impose on yourself relocations where you will change the place where you practice your activity. It could be a place of silence and focus, such as a new café, an unexplored quiet corner of your house, or a natural setting like a park or forest. Often, artists choose specific places of retreat for significant projects, such as a new book, a new series of artworks, or even to prepare for a sports competition.

A fresh new environment stimulates new inspiration and creativity, which is inevitably reflected in your work. Choose new locations specifically for their characteristics, such as a busy city if you are creating around the concept of excitement, or a quiet piece of countryside for developing an upcoming wellness program.

Major international companies understand this well. Take *Airbnb*, for example: its San Francisco office is centered around hospitality and community, with famous listings inspiring its meeting rooms and a playful design focused on wellness and Zen.

Alternatively, consider *Pixar*'s office in Emeryville, where powerful colors drawn from its movies create an immersive environment that stimulates creativity.

Use the environment to your advantage!

143

Passion Rituals

Creating recurring moments that keep your passion alive

PRACTICE

Let Earth Inspire Your Expression

📅 **QUARTERLY**   🕐 **ON GOING**

If you're a creative person seeking inspiration, what can be a better source than nature? It may be overheard, but Mother Earth is the most incredible artist. Traveling landscapes around your home, or far away abroad, stimulates that understanding to higher heights every time we do it.

Practicing your art and passion in general, taking inspiration from nature, encourages a deep connection with the elements.

At the start of each season, choose a theme, palette, or mood inspired by this specific season and the look of nature. For example, you could paint in warm Earthen tones in autumn or write outdoors about love in spring without sounding too cliche.

Collect elements across the seasons, draw inspiration from them, or even incorporate them into your creations to connect your work with the essence of these seasons.

If your passion is a sport, it could mean prioritizing beach runs and water-based workouts during the summer to stay in top physical shape.

Whatever it is, the point is for them to lead the way you practice your passion. At the end of each season, complete a closure ritual where you either display your work, share it with others, host a seasonal exhibition, or engage in a specific competition.

This habit encourages you to maintain a consistent thematic rhythm throughout the year and connect with nature in your daily activities.

Passion Rituals

Creating recurring moments that keep your passion alive

DEVELOPMENT

Allow Yourself to Reset

WEEKLY   **2 DAYS**

"If you do what you love, you won't have to work a day in your life."

This popular saying, often attributed to Confucius, the ancient Chinese philosopher, is undoubtedly true.

Your **passion** is a type of freedom that can overrule all other types. When you love doing something, **time** seems to stand still. The amount of **financial** earnings you make is no longer a factor. Being fully engaged with 100% of your **mental** capacity 100% of the time no longer feels like a burden. And being **physically** bound to a specific place becomes less of an inconvenience. At the same time, as you practice this passion to the fullest, your aura shines brighter, making you more beautiful in a **social** context, someone driven.

It is the freedom to rule them all.

In the chaos of practicing your passions with determinism, the greater risk is to lose yourself and forget to step back and think about what you do with more distance, allowing you to reconnect and clear your mind without worrying about productivity or efficiency.

Once a week, set aside a day for passive reflection on what truly animates you, to restore your mind and reconnect with yourself. Let your intuition guide you, temporarily setting aside progress, and enjoy your passion without pressure.

It might be revisiting old work, reading inspiring material, playing with unused tools, or planning future projects.

Resting and cultivating detachment allows your mind to breathe, develop curiosity, and foster strategic thinking, which, in turn, benefits the fruit of your passion.

ORIGAMI EDITIONS
READING FOR BETTER LIVING

THANK YOU!

We hope you enjoyed reading this book.

At **Origami Editions**, we trust that reading has the power to transform lives.

So, we publish books to help you:

✓ **Gain new life perspectives** by focusing on what matters
✓ **Grow business skills** to create lasting success
✓ **Become self-confident,** time-effective, and daring
✓ **Lead and inspire others,** becoming an effective leader

If you wish to discover our collections, follow our Author Page on Amazon:

And, if you want to be updated about new releases,
follow our social media:

Reading for Better Living!

For other inquiries, feel free to reach out to contact@origamieditions.com

Printed in Dunstable, United Kingdom